I0490978

THE CANCELLING OF
AMERICA:
WILL SHE SURVIVE?

JOHN D. SANDERSON

THE CANCELLING OF AMERICA: WILL SHE SURVIVE?

Copyright © 2021 John D. Sanderson.

All rights reserved. No part of this book may be used or reproduced by any means, graphic, electronic, or mechanical, including photocopying, recording, taping or by any information storage retrieval system without the written permission of the author except in the case of brief quotations embodied in critical articles and reviews.

iUniverse books may be ordered through booksellers or by contacting:

iUniverse
1663 Liberty Drive
Bloomington, IN 47403
www.iuniverse.com
844-349-9409

Because of the dynamic nature of the Internet, any web addresses or links contained in this book may have changed since publication and may no longer be valid. The views expressed in this work are solely those of the author and do not necessarily reflect the views of the publisher, and the publisher hereby disclaims any responsibility for them.

Any people depicted in stock imagery provided by Getty Images are models, and such images are being used for illustrative purposes only. Certain stock imagery © Getty Images.

ISBN: 978-1-6632-2602-0 (sc)
ISBN: 978-1-6632-2601-3 (e)

Library of Congress Control Number: 2021914411

Print information available on the last page.

iUniverse rev. date: 07/13/2021

Contents

Dedication

This book is dedicated to all the children in America with my prayers that the adult citizens of our country will take the actions necessary to prevent The Cancelling of America and preserve the last bastion of freedom in the world – the United States of America.

To my wife, Betty, without whose love, support, encouragement and, editorial assistance this work would not have been possible. And a special thanks to my daughter, Christy, for designing the cover for the book.

Prologue

I am ashamed to admit it, but until I was in my late 40s or early 50s, I did not pay much attention to the news. I would read the local newspaper, watch the local news and occasionally an evening news show on television. I paid close attention to what was happening in the country and world during the election season, but only focused on one or two issues that were important to me.

That is why I am writing this book. I know that younger people do not have time to dig into many issues be they local, state, national or worldwide. It takes many years to get your feet firmly on the ground. Marriage, children, and career occupy most of your waking hours when you are young. If you are married at 25 and have a child a year later, you are 48 years old before that child is out of college. Have a second or third child and you are in your 50s before you can focus on much else than family and career.

The audiences for this book are those people who care about our country but do not have the time to listen to multiple news outlets, and/ or research and read multiple publications. There are books galore that explore in detail any subject of interest. This is not one of those. My purpose is to provide a dose of information on many subjects and give some details that may be missed when listening to or reading a single news source. My objective is to provide a single source for the busiest people to gain a broad perspective of the issues impacting the future of our country.

Preface

The sky was crystal clear as I gazed at the stars – thousands, millions, no, billions of them twinkling through the jet-black emptiness between them. I thought back some 67 years when I was a tenderfoot Boy Scout on my first overnight campout. I was learning about the constellations to earn a merit badge. As I recall, I needed to earn five to get my second-class badge. I had not spent much time really looking at the stars since those worry-free days of my youthful innocence. As I lay on a comfortable lounge chair gazing skyward, I could still identify the Big Dipper, Little Dipper, Orion, Orion's Belt, and a few other celestial objects.

As best as I could remember, the sky looked tonight just as it did those decades ago. Yes, we know more about it today than we did then. The Hubble Space Telescope, the Space Station, the walk on the Moon and the Mars Rover, etc. have added vast amounts of knowledge about the space our tiny speck of the planet Earth floats around in. Despite all the advances in technology and knowledge, to the naked eye the sky looks the same.

I couldn't help but think how amazing it is that even though space is constantly expanding and changing, a certain order remains. The relationship between the Sun, Earth, Moon, and constellations I learned about as a kid in Indiana have remained stable and predictable for millions of years. I am equally amazed at how unstable our country has become as it has changed in just a couple of hundred years. It seems we have learned much through our scientific and technological advances about everything except governance. Greed and the quest for power are still the guiding principles of those we elect to political leadership.

The questions I am haunted by today are: Is America falling apart? Are we presently on the road to self-destruction like Rome? Can we bring America back together? Do a majority of citizens want it back?

As I explore those questions, I want to be fully transparent about my biases. I am American through and through. I stand when the American Flag passes. I stand for the National Anthem. I will kneel before God, but I will not kneel before BLM, Antifa, or any other cultural Marxist group. I have an ancestor, Richard Warren, who arrived on the Mayflower. I have relatives that fought in the Revolutionary War, fought for the North in the Civil War, and served in WW I, WW II, and the Korean conflict. I served as an Air Force medic in the Vietnam era and am proud of a grandson who recently served in the U.S. Army. I bleed red, white, and blue except when I watch Purdue University football and basketball games at which time my blood temporarily changes to Black and Gold.

I will attempt to present the most salient arguments on both sides of the issues, but I will also recommend actions for bringing America back to the people. Those that want to keep moving toward a big socialist style of government need only to do the opposite of my recommendations. I know the theory of socialism calls for the state to control production, distribution, and that exchange should be owned by the community. When I use the term in my writings, please think "central control." The government does not control everything yet, but it is getting closer with each passing day. I do not have the figures for 2021, but in 2016 we had 4,312 laws and 88,899 rules. Between the laws and the rules, government controls nearly every aspect of our lives.

.

Introduction
Crisis in America?

Whether we have a crisis in America is a matter of perspective and following the 2020 presidential election, it appears our country is divided down the middle between the Populists (focus on the people) and the Elites view (a class of people considered superior (by themselves and/or others). A serious clash of these opposing views could create a crisis approaching Civil War proportions. Lisa Wingate writes, "Every revolution starts with a spark on dry tinder."[1] The clash between Populists and Elitists has left us with a lot of dry timber and it is incumbent upon all of us to avoid creating the spark of revolution.

It is popular today to assign the Populists and the Elitists to the Republican and Democrat political parties. When I listen to our elected officials, and those who support them (especially financial supporters), I have come to believe that some of each exist in both political parties. Therefore, I will attempt to avoid using political party labels and stay with the Populist and Elitist designations, understanding, of course, that most people fall somewhere in the middle and would be appropriately described as moderate. The reality is, however, that it is the extreme Populists and the extreme Elitists that have the loudest voices, and they drown out the "silent" majority.

The conflicts today are not just about politics. They are not just about Republicans versus Democrats. They are not about the extremist views. What they are about is freedom, freedom of speech, liberty, the pursuit of happiness, the Constitution and our children's future.

---

[1] The Book of Lost Friends, "fiction" Large Print edition, Lisa Wingate (Random House) 2020, 37.

Let us start with a little refresher regarding what drove our founding fathers to form our government. We get a fairly good idea of what they wanted to accomplish in the preamble to the Declaration of Independence.

"We hold these truths to be self-evident, that all men are created equal, that they are endowed by their Creator with certain unalienable Rights, that among these are Life, Liberty and the pursuit of Happiness."[2] The Declaration goes on to detail the rationale for absolving allegiance to the British rule. If you want to read the entire document, I recommend going to the National Archives at https://www.archives.gov/founding-docs.

Now let us move to the Constitution.

"We the People of the United States, in Order to form a more perfect Union, establish justice, insure domestic Tranquility, provide for the common defense, promote the general Welfare, and secure the Blessings of Liberty to ourselves and our posterity, do ordain and establish this Constitution for the United States of America."[3]

"There are seven main articles in the Constitution that, in short, address the following:

1. Define the powers of the Congress, House of Representatives and Senate.
2. Establish and define the presidency.
3. Establish and define the court system.
4. Define states' laws.
5. Explain the Constitutional Amendment process.
6. Define the Constitution as the highest law in the country.
7. Explain what it would take to ratify the original document: nine of the 13 colonies had to agree to it.

The rest of the Constitution is created by amendments."[4]

"On September 25, 1789, the First Congress of the United States proposed 12 amendments to the Constitution. Ten of those proposed 12 amendments were ratified by three-fourths of the state legislatures on

---

[2] Preamble to the Declaration of Independence, National Archives.
[3] Preamble to the United States Constitution, National Archives.
[4] Https://www.enotes.com/homework-help/what-are-the-main-points-of-the-us-constitution-438124.

December 15, 1791. The ratified articles constitute the first 10 amendments of the Constitution, or the U.S. Bill of Rights."[5] I am including the Bill of Rights in its entirety as they are prominent in the conflicts within our country today.

Amendment I

Congress shall make no law respecting an establishment of religion, or prohibiting the free exercise thereof; or abridging the freedom of speech, or of the press; or the right of the people peaceably to assemble, and to petition the Government for a redress of grievances.

Amendment II

A well regulated Militia, being necessary to the security of a free State, the right of the people to keep and bear Arms shall not be infringed.

Amendment III

No Soldier shall, in time of peace be quartered in any house, without the consent of the Owner, nor in time of war, but in a manner to be prescribed by law.

Amendment IV

The right of the people to be secure in their persons, houses, papers, and effects, against unreasonable searches and seizures, shall not be violated, and no Warrants shall issue, but upon probable cause, supported by Oath or affirmation, and particularly describing the place to be searched, and the persons or things to be seized.

---

[5] The Bill of Rights, National Archives.

Amendment V

No person shall be held to answer for a capital, or otherwise infamous crime, unless on a presentment or indictment of a Grand Jury, except in cases arising in the land or naval forces, or in the Militia, when in actual service in time of War or public danger; nor shall any person be subject for the same offence to be twice put in jeopardy of life or limb; nor shall be compelled in any criminal case to be a witness against himself, nor be deprived of life, liberty, or property, without due process of law; nor shall private property be taken for public use, without just compensation.

Amendment VI

In all criminal prosecutions, the accused shall enjoy the right to a speedy and public trial, by an impartial jury of the State and district wherein the crime shall have been committed, which district shall have been previously ascertained by law, and to be informed of the nature and cause of the accusation; to be confronted with the witnesses against him; to have compulsory process for obtaining witnesses in his favor, and to have the Assistance of Counsel for his defense.

Amendment VII

In Suits at common law, where the value in controversy shall exceed twenty dollars, the right of trial by jury shall be preserved, and no fact tried by a jury, shall be otherwise re-examined in any Court of the United States, than according to the rules of the common law.

Amendment VIII

Excessive bail shall not be required, nor excessive fines imposed, nor cruel and unusual punishments inflicted.

Amendment IX

The enumeration in the Constitution, of certain rights, shall not be construed to deny or disparage others retained by the people.

Amendment X

The powers not delegated to the United States by the Constitution, nor prohibited by it to the States, are reserved to the States respectively, or to the people.

Since 1791 there have been an additional 17 amendments to the Constitution, and I will include some of those as they may apply in discussions later in the book. I will refer to these and other amendments and the seven articles in the Constitution as appropriate. For the complete original text of the Constitution, I refer you to archives.gov.

Sigmund Freud said, "Most people do not really want freedom, because freedom involves responsibility, and most people are frightened of responsibility."[6] At the 2018 Conservative Leadership Conference, Dennis Prager claimed, "Most Americans don't yearn for freedom but want to be taken care of."[7] These views conflict with the traditional American values I was raised to believe. That is, you are responsible for yourself – what you do, what you say, whether you succeed or fail, obey the law, or break the law, etc. You only need to look in a mirror to see who is to blame for your circumstances. I acknowledge that was certainly not true in the time of slavery, indentured servitude and more recently for those living under segregation and Jim Crow laws. Discrimination has also been experienced by other groups like the Italians and Polish but despite the discrimination, there are thousands of examples of those individuals that have not allowed it to deter them and through hard work and determination have achieved extreme successes in their lives. They took care of themselves. They did not ask others to take care of them.

---

[6] Civilization and its Discontents, "non-fiction" Sigmund Freud, 1930.
[7] Conservative Leadership Conference, "speech" Dennis Prager, April 14, 20178.

Do you want to give up your freedom and succumb to the will of others to take care of you? Only you can make that decision, but if you want to be taken care of, only make that decision for yourself and do not participate in forcing your choice on others.

CHAPTER ONE

Imperfections

My attempts to obtain permission to use some of the lyrics from the song, "All of Me" written by John Stephens/Toby Gad and sung by John Legend were unsuccessful. If you do not know the song, I encourage you to go online and listen to it. My interpretation of the lyrics is that you can love and give yourself to someone despite imperfections they may possess.

To me, that interpretation applies as much to America today as it does to the person the song is being sung to. To that person it means whatever you, I, or others might see as an imperfection, does not change my love for you. I will still give you everything I have, and you will give me everything you have.

America is not perfect. It never has been and most likely never will be. That does not mean you should give up on her. If you protect all that is good in her, America will give you the opportunity to do and be whatever you want.

I do not subscribe to Senator and presidential candidate Barack Obama's position stated on October 30, 2008, when he said, "We are five days away from fundamentally transforming the United States of America." Neither do I think it says anything positive about America when Senator Schumer celebrated the November 3, 2020, election by telling a New York crowd, "Now we take Georgia, then we change America." We should, and must, continue to work on improving America's imperfections but, as the old saying goes, "Don't throw the baby out with the bath water."

Maris Salazar, the newly elected Congresswoman for Florida's 27th District stated, "I was born in Little Havana in Miami to parents who fled Cuba with just $5 in their pocket, a taste of freedom, and the hope of building their own American Dream. Being raised in Miami and Puerto Rico, I grew up being told stories of the oppressive, Fidel Castro-led regime in Cuba, from which my parents and many from our community escaped. This experience forged in me the importance of liberty and profound pride for the United States of America, but it also made me aware of the fragility of freedom. Furthermore, she said that the powerful observation that President Ronald Regan once made about freedom rings true for me on an extremely personal level: 'Freedom is never more than one generation away from extinction. We did not pass it to our children in the bloodstream. It must be fought for, protected, and handed on for them to do the same.'

She additionally stated that "as a reporter, I focused on uncovering and exposing oppressive Communist and Socialist regimes across Latin America – including three years reporting from a Central American war zone in El Salvador. It was one of the most formative and powerful experiences of my life, but one moment stands above all the rest – when I stood up to and challenged Fidel Castro in his first interview on American soil. That day, I saw the face of socialism personified, and I faced the evil that tormented my family and countless others."[8]

Britannica defines Socialism as, "a social and economic doctrine that calls for public rather than private ownership or control of property and natural resources. According to the socialist view, individuals do not live or work in isolation but live in cooperation with one another. Furthermore, everything that people produce is in some sense a social product, and everyone who contributes to the production of a good is entitled to a share in it. Society as a whole, therefore, should own or at least control property for the benefit of all its members. This conviction puts socialism in direct opposition to capitalism, which is based on private ownership of the means of production and allows individual choices in a free market to determine how goods and services are distributed. Socialists complain that capitalism necessarily leads to unfair and exploitative concentrations of wealth and power in the hands of the relatively few who emerge victorious from free-market competition – people who then use their wealth and power to

---

[8] Secure.winter.com/Salazar/action-127936.

reinforce their dominance in society. Because such people are rich, they may choose where and how to live, and their choices in turn limit the options of the poor. As a result, terms such as individual freedom and equality of opportunity may be meaningful to capitalists but can only ring hollow for working people, who must do the capitalists' bidding if they are to survive. As socialists see it, true freedom and true equality require social control of the resources that provide the basis for prosperity in any society."[9]

Our government does not yet have control of the resources that provide the basis for prosperity in society, but I fear it is moving closer and closer as years, and now, even days and weeks, pass. Controls are ever increasing on land use, exploration for oil and gas, agriculture, energy production, manufacturing, and transportation to name a few.

Our freedom of speech is being infringed as big tech companies censor posts and the mainstream media refuses to report on news that conflicts with their beliefs. When my wife asked a friend living in Chicago about the shootings and killings on the Southside and demonstrations in the inner city, she was astounded to hear him say he thought everything in the city was fine – he had not seen anything disturbing about those issues in the news. Was it not being fully reported, or did he think it was fake news? Maybe such violence has become so commonplace that it is now a normal part of life. Incredibly sad if that is the case.

Our universities should be bastions for free speech. "If only Stanford University agreed! The high-profile California school has come under scrutiny in recent years for anti-free-speech incidents, from the roadblocks it created for conservative student groups that wanted to host conservative speakers to the Faculty Senate's sustained efforts to silence Hoover Institution fellows for daring to argue outside the narrow confines of far-left ideology."[10]

From the desk of Ann Coulter: "A student group asked me to speak about our nation's immigration laws at the University of California at Berkeley, the so-called 'birthplace of the free speech movement.' As you

---

[9] Britannica.com; Richard Dagger, Professor of Political Science, Arizona State University, Tempe.
[10] Stand up for free speech at Stanford University, Nicole Neily, Speech First, now@ readactnews.com, February 5, 2021.

may have heard, my speech was abruptly canceled because leftist thugs decided to riot and the administration wouldn't stick up for free speech."[11]

I think our founding fathers would roll over in their graves if they knew about the following:

- A fence with razor wire around the Capitol along with armed military in Washington, D.C.
- It took more than 90 days after the election for New York's 22nd Congressional District to declare a winner.
- People are losing their jobs because they disagree with the prevailing political positions.
- President Biden is now considering a commission to study changes to the Supreme Court that could lead to increasing the number of justices and "packing the court" with justices supportive of administration policies.

Those are but a few of the things being supported by those that believe America needs to be transformed. Yet, according to a 2018 Gallup poll, about 158,000,000 adults worldwide would migrate to the United States if they could.[12] Millions more try to stream across the southern border from Mexico to gain entry to the United States and the benefits and opportunities that await them.

If America is in such need of transformation, why do so many want to come here?

Is America falling apart because it is such a bad country or is it being torn apart by those that do not like the freedoms and opportunities we have? Is it just a power grab by the elite? Is it that people do not want freedom but really want to be taken care of? In the chapters that follow, I will address the imperfections some believe call for America's transformation and how we can make changes without destroying the country.

---

[11] College campuses have gone insane, Ann Coulter, Alert.keep americagreatness. com, February 4, 2021.

[12] More Than 750 Million Worldwide Would Migrate If They Could, Gallup, Neil Esipova, Anita Pugliese and Julie Ray, December 10, 2018.

ACTIONS

1. When thinking about America's imperfections also take some time to think about America's goodness. Things like the freedom to live where you want, how you want; freedom to work and advance in your occupation; the opportunity to dream big and work to make that dream a reality.

2. When you listen to people talk about what they believe needs to be done to improve an imperfection, encourage them to recognize that there may be multiple approaches to the problem and that each approach has its positive and negative components.

3. Be open to considering other points of view. If you do not listen to others, especially those you disagree with, you will surely develop tunnel vision and will not consider the potential downside of a given position.

4. Watch a news program you do not like at least once a week. If your main source of information is CNN, MSNBC, or other stations with a left bias, watch a show on FOX News like Tucker Carlson. For good discussions about the Constitution, you should give Life, Liberty & Levin a try once a month or so. If you only watch FOX News, tune in to one of the left-leaning networks. You may disagree with what you see and hear, but you will learn the position of "the other side." You will be prepared to participate in a more meaningful debate if you know the rationale for your opponent's position and will be better equipped with facts to counter it.

CHAPTER TWO

Where are We Headed?

Since it has been about 60 years since I read it, I just re-read George Orwell's "1984." For those who read the book here is a brief recap. In the year 1984, Orwell imagines a society ruled by "Big Brother" the public face of the government. There are 4 ministries, and they are named after the opposite of their true functions – doublethink.

The Ministry of Peace concerns itself with war against other super states.

The Ministry of Love identifies, monitors, arrests, and converts real and imagined dissidents. This is where the Thought Police beat and torture dissidents, after which they are sent to Room 101 to face "the worst things in the world" – until love for Big Brother and the Party replaces dissension.

The Ministry of Truth controls information: news, entertainment, education, and the arts. This is where historical records are altered to make Big Brother's current statements appear to be true.

The Ministry of Plenty controls food, goods and domestic production and changes historical records to support their claims of increased rations.[13]

The story (published in 1949) takes place in 1984 and centers on the consequences of totalitarianism, mass surveillance, and the repressive regimentation of persons and behaviors within society. Civilization has been damaged by war, civil conflict, and revolution. Airstrip One (formerly Great Britain) is a province of Oceania, one of three super-states that rule the world. It is ruled by the "Party" under the mysterious leader Big

---

[13] 1984, "social science fiction," George Orwell, Secker & Warburg, 1949.

Brother. The Party brutally purges out anyone who does not fully conform to their regime using the Thought Police and constant surveillance through Telescreens (two-way televisions), cameras, and hidden microphones. Those who fall out of favor with the Party become "in persons," disappearing with all evidence of their existence destroyed.

The main character, Winston Smith, works in the Ministry of Truth where he rewrites historical records to conform to the state's ever-changing version of history. He is eventually identified as a "thought criminal," sent to Room 101 where he is tortured in the final stage of re-education.[14] As is the fate of all who undergo re-education, he is killed with a bullet to the back of the head and all evidence of his existence is erased. If you have not read the book, you should.

Today, "Cancel Culture" is a form of ostracism in which someone is thrust out of social or professional circles. "Big Tech" monitors us online and through social media. Politicians lie, investigative journalism has disappeared from broadcast and print media, and those that disagree with the left-leaning party line are censored.

We may not be living in the world of "1984" but we are approaching it at a rate extremely uncomfortable for me and I believe about 75 million other citizens.

"Rules for Radicals" is a 1971 book by community activist Saul D. Alinsky. It was a guide for communities to gain, through any means necessary, social, political, legal, and economic power. On the 4th fly-leaf page of his book he includes the following:

> Lest we forget an over-the-shoulder acknowledgment to the very first radical: from all our legends, mythology, and history (and who is to know where mythology leaves off and history begins – or which is which), the first known to man who rebelled against the establishment and did it so effectively that he at least won his own kingdom – Lucifer.[15]

---

[14] HTTPS://en.m.Wikipedia.org/wiki/Nineteen_Eighty_Four.
[15] Https://en.m.Wikipedia.org/wiki/Rules_for_Radicals.

Alinsky would draw on loyalty to a particular structured organization (church or religious affiliation for example) with which to operate because they were easier to mobilize. Once the organization was united behind something he would find a common enemy for the community to be united against. He would then find an external antagonist to turn into a "common enemy" for the community. This was often a local politician or agency. The use of conflict allowed for the goal of the community to be clearly defined – defeat the enemy. He encouraged over-the-top public demonstrations that could not be ignored, and these tactics enabled the organization to reach their goals faster than through the normal bureaucratic process.

The "Rules" are:

1. Power is not only what you have but what the enemy thinks you have.
2. Never go outside the expertise of your people.
3. Whenever possible go outside the expertise of the enemy.
4. Make the enemy live up to its own book of rules.
5. Ridicule is man's most potent weapon. There is no defense. It is almost impossible to counterattack ridicule. Also, it infuriates the opposition, who then react to your advantage.
6. A good tactic is one you or people enjoy.
7. A tactic that drags on too long becomes a drag.
8. Keep the pressure on.
9. The threat is usually more terrifying than the thing itself.
10. The major premise for tactics is the development of operations that will maintain a constant pressure upon the opposition.
11. If you push a negative hard and deep enough it will break through into its counter side; this is based on the principle that every positive has its negatives.
12. The price of a successful attack is a constructive alternative.
13. Pick the target, freeze it, personalize it, and polarize it.[16]

Jean Chen reported on a YouTube video of a 1985 interview of Yuri Bezmenov, a KGB agent who defected to the West in 1970. The interview

---

[16] Ibid.

is about the Soviet Union's strategy to subvert the United States. He states: "Marxism-Leninism ideology is being pumped into the soft heads of at least three generations of American students, without being challenged or counter-balanced by the basic values Americanism and American patriotism...The demoralization process in the United States is basically completed already...Most of it is done by Americans to Americans thanks to a lack of moral standards. As I mentioned before, exposure to true information does not matter anymore. A person who was demoralized is unable to assess true information. The facts tell nothing to him. Even if I shower him with information, with authentic proof, with documents, with pictures. Even if I take him by force to the Soviet Union and show him concentration camps, he will refuse to believe it until he is going to receive a kick in his fat bottom. When the military boot crashes him, then he will understand, but not before that. That's the tragic of the situation of demoralization."[17]

Bezmenov said subversion happens in four stages: demoralization, destabilization, crisis, and normalization. The first stage lasts about 15-20 years, the time needed to raise a generation, is to brainwash the public with communist ideology. Manipulation of the media and academia is required for this purpose.

The second stage focuses on throwing society into chaos, and it usually takes 2-5 years. During this stage, the status quo in economy, foreign relations, and defense systems are changed. The establishment promises all kinds of goodies to win people's support for creating a massive government that is intrusive to people's lives.

The third stage instigates a crisis that leads to civil war, revolution, or foreign invasion. This stage only took 2-6 months. This is the stage when the leftist idealists, or "useful idiots," are no longer needed, because they would be disillusioned and become obstacles. They are going to be eliminated, exiled, or imprisoned, such as what happened in Grenada, Afghanistan, Bangladesh, and China.

The final stage, normalization, can take up to 20 years to complete – the populace begins to accept and assimilate communism.[18]

[17] Looking Through an Adversary's Eyes: A KGB Agent's Prophecy, Jean Chen, The Epoch Times, Opinion & Business, January 20-26, 2021.
[18] Ibid.

Bezmenov said, "The United States is in a state of war. Undeclared total war against the basic principles and the foundation of this system… The time bomb is ticking. Every second, the disaster is coming closer and closer. Unlike myself, you will have nowhere to defect to unless you want to live in Antarctica with penguins. This is it. This is the last country of freedom and possibility."[19]

How did we get here so quickly without anyone talking about it?

Those wanting to transform America will not campaign for full-blown communism or socialism but will start with Oligarchy, a form of power structure in which power rests with a small number of people. That can be put in place without people even noticing. Fact is, we are there now. George Bernard Shaw defined in his play "Major Barbara" a new type of Oligarchy – the intellectual oligarchy that acts against the interests of the common people: "I now want to give the common man weapons against the intellectual man. I love the common people. I want to arm them against the lawyer, the doctor, the priest, the literary man, the professor, the artist, and the politician, who, once in authority, are the most dangerous, disaster out and tyrannical of all the fools, rascals, and imposters. I want a democratic power strong enough to force the intellectual oligarchy to use its genius for the general good or else parish."[20]

Jean Chen's article also includes the following: John Adams said: "Our Constitution was made only for a moral and religious people. It is wholly inadequate to the government of any other." She adds the following from ruthless communist dictator, Joseph Stalin who echoed his point from a different angle. "America is like a healthy body and its resistance is threefold: its patriotism, its morality, and its spiritual life. If we can undermine these three areas, America will collapse from within."[21]

During the summer of 2020 and the first quarter of 2021 we have experienced:

- Riots and destruction in Atlanta, Bakersfield, Boston, Chicago, Columbus, Dallas/Fort Worth, Des Moines, Denver, Detroit,

---

[19] Ibid.

[20] Shaw, Bernard und Brazilian, Vitaly. 2-in-1: English-German. Major Barbara & Majorin Barbara. New Youk, 2020, ISBN 979-8692881076.

[21] Looking Through an Adversary's Eyes: A KGB Agent's Prophecy, Jean Chen, The Epoch Times, Opinion & Business, January 20-26, 2021.

District of Columbia, Houston, Los Angeles, Louisville, Memphis, Minneapolis, New York City, Phoenix, Portland, Sacramento, San Jose, and Seattle. There are others but these suffice to make the point.

- Police stations and a Federal Court House have been taken over by demonstrators.
- Historic monuments have been torn down and/or defaced.
- The historic St. John's Episcopal Church was set on fire during protests.
- The Capitol Building was breached by protesters.
- Police have been shot and killed while sitting in their patrol cars.
- Speech has been censored
- People have lost jobs (been punished) because of their political beliefs.
- People are being monitored through social media, the television programs they watch, their credit card purchases, etc.
- The Corona virus pandemic has been politicized.
- The country has become severely divided over political and social justice issues.
- Those not agreeing with the predominate political beliefs are being vilified.

We see elements of Orwell's imagined society and Alinsky's "Rules" playing out to a greater extent each day. On January 15, 1987, Jesse Jackson and about 500 protesters marched down Palm Drive, Stanford University's grand main entrance, chanting "Hey, hey, ho, ho, Western Civ has got to go." That may be when manipulation of academics took hold in what Bezmenov called the "demoralization" stage of a takeover by Marxism-Leninism ideology. Bezmenov's second stage, throwing society into chaos and the promising of all kinds of goodies (free college, free healthcare, etc.) to win people's support is well underway. The biggest question today is: how far away are we from stage three – instigation of a crisis that leads to civil war or revolution?

I passionately believe that the question, "Where are We Headed" will be answered in the next 2-4 years. That determination will be made by you and every other American citizen. It will be made by what you believe, what you value, what you fight for and, most importantly, who you vote for. And vote you must! Voting is the most powerful tool you have to voice what you want America to be for you and your posterity. Thomas Jefferson said, "If we are to guard against ignorance and remain free, it is the responsibility of every American to be informed."

ACTIONS

1. Give serious thought to whether you want freedom or want to be taken care of. Regardless of what some politician may tell you, you cannot have both.
2. Educate yourself on the issues – do not just listen to biased sources.
3. Decide the America you want for your children, grandchildren, etc. Make the choices in the next 48 months (about 4 years) that draw you closer to the America you want for your descendants.
4. When deciding who to vote for, and it does not matter whether you are voting for a school board representative, local or state official, a representative, senator, or the president of the United States, do not listen as much to what they say during the election cycle, look at what they have said and done in the past. Politicians tend to say what they think you want to hear and that is not necessarily what they believe or will support once in office. That is sad but unfortunately true for far too many. For politicians currently in office, you can go to justfacts. votesmart.org and get information on them, their votes, positions, ratings, speeches, and funding. Funding is especially important because it will tell you what people or organizations that are likely to have an enormous influence on their votes.
5. Once you have decided who to vote for, support them. Tell others why you are supporting them. Put a yard sign on your property if you can. Give them a donation – it does not have to be a big one, $5, $10, or $25, whatever you can afford, but give something.

CHAPTER THREE

1619 & 1776

In chapter two I reviewed George Orwell's book "1984" and how the Ministry of Truth controls information and alters historical records to make Big Brother's statements appear to be true. Former KGB agent described the first stage of a Marxist-Leninist ideology as including the manipulation of the media. Saul Alinsky called for the identification of a common enemy and using over-the-top public demonstrations as a tool for defeating the enemy.

It seems to me that today the New York Times is acting as a "Ministry of Truth" in order to re-write history, create a common enemy and lay the groundwork for civil unrest with its "1619 Project." The Project teaches the primary reason people came to America was to prosper through slavery. It teaches Americans to hate America. There is a second option to consider - the patriotic history we have learned about all these years is wrong and the "1619 Project" represents the real history. But there is a third option that makes more sense to me – there is some truth in the 1619 message as well as that of our founding fathers. Multiple truths can coexist without invalidating each other. I will focus on the third option as I explore the wedge being driven between Americans by the "1619 Project."

European nations came to America to increase their wealth with the Spanish and Europeans among the first to explore the New World. "By 1650, however, England had established a dominant presence on the Atlantic coast. The first colony was founded at Jamestown, Virginia, in 1607. Many of the people who settled in the New World came to escape religious persecution. The Pilgrims, founders of Plymouth, Massachusetts arrived in 1620. In both Virginia and Massachusetts, the colonists flourished with some assistance from Native Americans."[22]

"The 1619 Project" is a journalism project by Nikole Hannah-Jones and writers from the New York Times and New York Times Magazine. It reframed America's history by placing the consequences of slavery at the center of the United States national story. It was published in August 2020 for the 400th anniversary of the arrival of the first enslaved Africans in England's Virginia Colony. Factually, this is incorrect. "The first enslaved African people arrived in North America in 1526."[23] "Slavery in North America extends to before the arrival of Europeans[24] and European slavery in the New World is documented as far back as Columbus in 1494, possibly as early as 1493."[25] "In 1619, African slaves arrived in the Colony of Virginia. A ship carrying 20-30 people who had been enslaved by a joint African-Portuguese war on Ndongo in modern Angola, landed at Point Comfort in the colony of Virginia."[26]

The first edition of the 1619 Project was published on August 14, 2019, and included the following:

- "America Wasn't a Democracy Until Black Americans Made it One, essay by Nikole Hannah-Jones.
- American Capitalism Is Brutal. You Can Trace That to the Plantation, Essay by Matthew Desmond.
- What the Reactionary Politics of 2019 Owe to the Politics of Slavery, Essay by Jamelle Bouie.

One of the central claims made by Hannah-Jones is that the colonists fought the Revolutionary War to preserve Slavery. The claim was later

---

[22] Http://www.America's library.gov/Jeb/colonial/jb_colonial_subj.html.

[23] Torres-Spelliscy, Ciara, Perspective – Everyone is talking about 1619. But that's not actually when slavery in America started, August 23, 2019.

[24] Snyder, Christina, 2010.

[25] Commentary, The Pulitzer Prizes. Columbia University, May 4, 2020.

[26] Nelson, Alexandria, The 1619 Project and the stories we tell about slavery, August 15, 2019.

softened to "some of" the colonists fought to preserve slavery. The essays further discuss details of history as well as modern American society."[27]

"Imagine a high school classroom where the history teacher asks the students how societal structures continue to support the enslavement of Black people. Then the conversation continues to dissect the role of slaves in the development of America, abandoning the predictable narrative of the Civil War, emancipation, freedom.

That curriculum exists. The Pulitzer Center helped turn The New York Times "The 1619 Project" into a curriculum that's now taught in more than 4,500 schools nationwide."[28]

"One recommended 'activity to extend student engagement' asks teachers to lead students in transforming historical documents through *erasure poetry*, which, the curriculum explains, can be a way of reclaiming and reshaping historical documents; they can lay bare the real purpose of the document or transform it into something wholly new. How will you highlight inequity – or envision liberation through your erasure poem? Students could, the guide suggests, erase parts of the Declaration to make it fit Hannah-Jones's essay or amend the Thirteenth Amendment to make it harmonize with an essay arguing that 'mass incarceration and excessive punishment is the legacy of slavery.'"[29]

Despite many of the claims in The 1619 Project having been debunked and later altered or softened in subsequent publications, it has been a major contributor to identity politics and oppression studies. "A professor at Columbia, John McWhorter, in perhaps the most perceptive of all the essays yet written about The 1619 Project, wrote in **Reason**, 'the 1619 idea joins many others in bolstering the black American soul with the substitute pride of noble victimhood. If you are a member of a race whose subjugation is part of the very DNA of the nation, it renders anything one does well a kind of victory snatched from the jaws of defeat (if only at

---

[27] HTTPS://en.m.Wikipedia.org/wiki/The_1619_project.

[28] HTTPS://www.Frederick news post.com/news/education/the_1619-p...old-has/article.a2921b75-d012-5e93-9816-8e76253f1d4.html.

[29] A Divisive, Historically Dubious Curriculum, Max Eden, City Journal, December 3, 2019.

generations' remove) and in general lends one a way of feeling significant, distinct, special."[30]

Before going further, let me say this – SLAVERY IN AMERICA WAS BAD AND IS STILL BAD WHEREVER IT EXISTS ANYWHERE IN THE WORLD! We need to openly acknowledge that it happened, is a black spot on our history, and racism has had a negative impact on black Americans. I'll write more about racism in another chapter.

"The **1776 Commission** was an advisory committee established in September 2020 by then-U.S. President Donald Trump to support what he called "patriotic education"[31] The commission was a response to the 1619 Project. "According to the executive order establishing the commission, the commission's goal was to end what it calls the "radicalized view of American history" which has "vilified (the United States') Founders and (its) founding."[32] The "patriotic education" was also aimed at refuting critical race theory. "The commission was also intended to promote these concepts at national parks, landmarks, and monuments among other federal properties; federal agencies were instructed to provide grants and initiatives in a way that prioritized those supporting the American founding."[33] The commission's report was released on January 18, 2021, and identified progressivism, racism, and identity politics as "challenges to America's principles." The report was criticized by historians and just hours after his inauguration, President Joe Biden issued an executive order dissolving the 1776 commission and the report was removed from the Whitehouse website.

I concede that both the 1619 project and the 1776 commission report contain historical inaccuracies or misrepresentations. Both come from biased perspectives. However, both also contain accurate information. Everyone should support the goal of teaching students an accurate and

[30] HTTPS://www.educationnext.org/1619-project-enters-American-classrooms-adding-new-sizzle-slavery-significant-cost/.

[31] Crowley, Michael; Schuessler, Jennifer (January 19,2021). "Trump's 1776 Commission Critiques Liberalism in Report Derided by Historians" The New York Times. ISSN 0362-4331.

[32] Trump, Donald J. (November 2, 2020). "Executive Order on Establishing the President's Advisory 1776 Commission" Whitehouse.gov.

[33] Guadiana, Nicole (November 11, 2020). "Trump creates 1776 Commission to promote 'patriotic education'" Politico, November 24, 2020.

unbiased history of America. I, for one, am among I believe many who believe America began in 1776 - not 1492, 1619 or any other date other than 1776. I covered our founding documents in the introduction to the book and will not repeat them here. I will say our founding fathers created a remarkable country and that although it may be imperfect, it is still the best country in the world to live in. I believe, however, that many in our country, including some in the U.S. House of Representatives and U.S. Senate, just do not like America and the Republic for which it stands.

This is what many Americans are seeing now:

- We have athletes protesting by kneeling for the national anthem.
- We have the owner of a professional basketball team saying they will not play the national anthem at home games.
- When Representative Matt Gaetz (R-FL) proposed to have a committee open its meetings with the Pledge of Allegiance, the Democrats voted it down.
- We now have a president that does not want to encourage "patriotism."

To me, those actions are un-American. They fly in the face of why we fought the Revolutionary War.

ACTIONS

1. Get involved with your children's schools.
2. For a detailed response to the 1619 project, read, <u>1620 A Critical Response to the 1619 Project</u>, by Peter W. Wood.
3. Learn all you can about what your children are being taught.
4. Get to know those running for your school boards. Be sure their primary concern is the students and that they are not shills for special interests.
5. Help your children to understand both the good and terrible things in our history.

6. Teach your children the proper ways to work to improve America but caution against throwing the baby out with the bath water.
7. Show you are proud of America – stand for the national anthem and fly the American flag if you can.
8. Financially support and vote for officials that reflect American values.

CHAPTER FOUR

Government Overreach

The Declaration of Independence includes the following: We hold these truths to be self-evident, that all Men are created equal, that they are endowed by the Creator with certain unalienable Rights, that among these are Life, Liberty, and the Pursuit of Happiness – That to secure these Rights, *Governments are instituted among Men, deriving their just Powers from the Consent of the Governed* (emphasis added) ...

I understand that the Declaration of Independence is not a legal document, but the intent of our founders is quite clear - that the Government gets its powers form the consent of the governed.

The preamble to the Constitution defines the role of the Federal Government as establishing justice, insuring domestic tranquility, providing for the common defense, promoting the general welfare, and securing the blessings of Liberty to ourselves and our posterity. That is, IT. Our founders knew that governments have a propensity to grow, and they passed the Bill of Rights to ensure the government does not grow big and powerful enough to trample all over the citizens.

I attempted to identify the number of federal agencies that exist, but it is an extremely elusive number, and if an authoritative list exists, I have not been able to find it. I did find the following from a 2015 article: "FOIA.gov (maintained by the Department of Justice) lists 78 independent executive agencies and 174 components of the executive departments as units that comply with the Freedom of Information Act requirements imposed on every federal agency. The U.S. Government Manual lists

96 independent executive units and 220 components of the executive departments. USA.gov, lists 137 independent executive agencies and 268 units in the Cabinet"[34]

In his book, The Road to Serfdom, F.A. Hayek writes, "The power which a multiple millionaire, who may be my neighbour and perhaps my employer, has over me is very much less than that which the smallest fonctionnaire possesses who wields the coercive power of the state, and on whose discretion it depends whether and how I am to be allowed to live or to work."[35]

A principle that defines America is the Rule of Law. I found several definitions for "law" but they are all similar in nature. Here is one from Merriam-Webster: "a binding custom or practice of a community: a rule of conduct or action prescribed or formally recognized as binding or enforced by a controlling entity. The courts exist to uphold, interpret, and apply the law." In short, a law is set of instructions which tells us the way things are to be done. They are created by elected officials (government), enforced by police and prosecutors, with pre-determined consequences for a specific behavior or act, and the consequences are fixed.[36] Between 1995 and 2016 our Federal Government enacted 4,313 laws.

But laws are not the only things governing our behavior. There are Rules. Like law, rules are a set of instructions which tells us the way things are to be done. But that is where the similarities end. Rules are created by individuals. Rules are enforced by those creating the rules. The consequences of rules vary and are flexible depending on circumstances of the behavior or act.[37] Between 1995 and 2016 the federal government published 88,899 rules. It is the rule makers and rule enforcers that Hayek was referring to in The Road to Serfdom.

Federal rulemaking is the mechanism through which the federal government implements policies. According to the Office of the Federal Register the number of final rules published each year is generally in the

---

[34] https://cei.org/blog/nobody-knows-how-many-federal-agencies-exist/, Crews, Clyde Wayne, 8/26/2015.

[35] The Road to Serfdom, Haye, F.A., University of Chicago Press, September 18, 1944.

[36] https://sumnerpc.com/rules-vs-laws/.

[37] Ibid.

range of 3,000-4,500. In 2018, approximately 25% of the total pages of the *Federal Register* were in the "Rules and Regulations" section.

Bureaucracies are run by non-elected government employees and implement federal laws enacted by Congress. They write the rules and regulations that affect our lives. Bureaucracies exist in all levels of government, federal, state, and local, but I will be focusing on the federal bureaucracy because it is the biggest and has the most impact on us.

The federal bureaucracy includes 15 executive departments, which come together in the president's cabinet. These departments are organized into independent executive agencies, independent regulatory agencies, government corporations, and presidential commissions. These organizations include: Department of Agriculture (USDA - 1862), Department of Commerce (DOC - 1903), Department of Defense (DOD - 1947), Department of Education (ED - 1979), Department of Energy (DOE - 1977), Department of Health and Human Services (HHS - 1953), Department of Homeland Security (DHS - 2002), Department of Housing and Urban Development (HUD -1965), Department of the Interior (DOI - 1849), Department of Justice (DOJ -1870), Department of Labor (DOL - 1913), Department of State (DOS - 1789), Department of Transportation (DOT - 1967), Department of Treasury (TREAS - 1789), and the Department of Veterans Affairs (VA - 1930).[38]

I wrote earlier about the difficulty in identifying the number of federal agencies that exist making it impossible for me to estimate the number of non-elected bureaucrats writing, implementing, and enforcing the thousands of rules. Suffice it to say, there are a bunch of them and as my grandmother would have said, there is a hunch-a-bunch of them.

We are not only controlled by the laws passed by congress and the rules written by bureaucrats. Governance now is by Executive Fiat. For example, as of March 19, 2021, President Joe Biden had signed 37 Executive Orders, 13 Presidential Memoranda (similar to Executive Orders, but do not have the same publication requirements), 17 Proclamations, and seven Notices. They are issued at the discretion of the President and not subject to discussion in or vote by Congress. If the President's actions are part of his campaign promises, then they can be construed to have the consent

---

[38] https://examples.yourdictionary.com/federal-bureaucracy-examples-in-everyday-life.html.

of the people. However, presidents are free to issue Executive Orders and Memoranda on issues not discussed during the campaign that are diametrically opposed to campaign promises and/or public opinion.

We are also impacted by Judicial Activism which is a philosophy in which judges allow their personal views about public policy to guide their decisions - the 1973 case of Roe v. Wade in which the Supreme Court created a constitutional right to abortion may be the most famous example.

All these laws, rules, regulations, and executive orders have led to an astounding growth in government and government spending. In 1990, the government spent $4,760 per person and in 2020 it spent $19,962. In 2000 the government spent 18% of the Gross Domestic Product (GDP) and it rose to 44% in 2020. Federal health care expenditures were $156 billion in 1990 and $4 trillion in 2020. On March 1, 2021, the national debt was $28 trillion and that translates to $84,834 per person and $216,933 per household.

With the government intimately involved in virtually every aspect of our lives, it is no wonder that respect for government service and public servants is declining. In an April 2019 Pew Research Center poll, only 17% of respondents said they trusted the federal government "to do the right thing." Even though trust in the federal government is incredibly low, a majority of respondents thought the size of government is about right while 47% see government as either too big or too small. The poll showed that 67% of those who affiliate with the Democratic Party express support for the expansion of government services while 74% of those who affiliate with the Republican Party want the government to shrink.[39] We truly are a divided America!

This brings me back to Dennis Prager's claim that "Most Americans don't yearn for freedom but want to be taken care of." Evidence seems to be pointing in the direction of people wanting to be taken care of, and if that is the case, the America of freedom and liberty is on the verge of extinction. So, what kind of country do we have today?

During his March 21, 2021, television show, Life, Liberty and Levin, Mark Levin analyzed it this way (paraphrased). Is it a federation of states with a republican form of government (federal republic)? Not really. We are

---

[39] https://www.brookings.edu/policy2020/votervital/public-service-and-the-federal-government/.

moving toward more centralization of authority in the federal government. More of an authoritarian state.

Are we a representative republic? With the far-reaching arms of our bureaucrats, we do not have much say about anything.

Are we a constitutional republic? Not really. Most of the constitutional firewalls have been breached and the Supreme Court does not enforce the constitution.

How did we get here? It is because our freedom and liberty have eroded over an extended period. It is like the boiling frog fable. If you put a frog in a pot of boiling water, it will jump out. However, if the frog is placed in tepid water that is then brought to a boil slowly, the frog will not perceive the danger and it will be cooked to death.

Without freedom and liberty, tyranny is not far away. Do the citizens of America want a government in which all power is in the hands of the federal government, unelected bureaucrats, the corporate and political elites? Do we want to be cooked to death?

ACTIONS

1. Start paying close attention to what is going on in Washington, D.C.
2. Think for yourself. Do not just listen to a single source of information.
3. Get involved in the elections of your congressmen and senators.
4. Demand that the media make a careful and critical examination of political candidates and proposed legislation.
5. Nothing is 100%. All legislation will have some elements that you like, but it is extremely important to understand the long-term implications for both the elements you like and those you dislike.
6. Do not be so blinded by the promise of "goodies" that you overlook everything else.

CHAPTER FIVE

Woke & Cancel Culture

I admit it, I am old. I am so old that I thought "Woke" meant "not falling asleep." I have been hearing about "wokeness" a lot over the past few years and while looking into it I learned how out-of-touch I was. Now I know that "Woke," according to the Oxford dictionary, means "alert to injustice in society, especially racism." Okay, I am old, but not too old to learn.

I am including "Cancel Culture" in this chapter because as I was learning about Woke, I also learned that if I disagree with those that declare a position as Woke, then it is okay for me to be "Cancelled." In other words, it is okay for me to be made a social outcast, shunned, and even prevented from earning a living if I am not woke. There goes freedom of thought and expression, and, with that, goes one of the pillars that makes America so special – even exceptional.

As I thought about it, I thought I had been Woke (by the current definition) most of my adult life. I have to say adult life because until I graduated from high school and entered the real world, I knew little to nothing about struggles of Black Americans.

I grew up in a small town in Indiana and I only knew one Black American. He was four years ahead of me in school, so I did not know him well. I do not remember his first name, but his nickname was "Beany." He got this nickname while on a Boy Scout camp out when he placed a can of beans on the fire but forgot to punch a hole in the top to let the steam out. The can exploded covering him with beans, hence, the nickname "Beany." Beany was in my older sister's class, and I remember her, and many others who knew him, saying what a great guy he was and how everyone liked him. I did not have any reason to harbor any biases toward Black Americans at that time in my life.

My understanding of the mistreatment of Black Americans began about 1960. A farmer in a county adjacent to mine hired a Black American tenant (Mr. Davis) to farm his land. The farmer's land was in White County and Mr. Davis was not allowed to live in White County, so the farmer bought a house for him in my county, Carroll County. I was working part time at a service station and tire dealership and Mr. Davis always came to us for tires, tire repairs, vehicle service, etc. That is how I got to know him. He was a delightful man to serve whenever he came into the shop, and I always thought it was so wrong that he could not live in White County.

When I was a freshman at Purdue University in 1961, Johnny Mathis came to campus for a series of performances. I was shocked to learn he was not allowed to stay in the Purdue Memorial Union Hotel because he was black. He stayed in one of the fraternities on campus. An unrelated side note here. My word processing program just informed me that I was not a freshman but first-year-student. Political Correctness has gone bonkers. I was a freshman.

After college I began my healthcare career in a hospital clinical and pathology laboratory. I began working with Black Americans and other people of color. They were all very competent, hardworking, and friendly. I learned very quickly that regardless of a person's color, their blood was still red, their blood cells all looked the same, their internal organs and tissues were the same. The only difference was the color of their skin – and where they lived!

In the mid to late 1960s, the Black American population of Tippecanoe County Indiana (where my hospital was located) was about 800 and most of them lived in the few blocks surrounding the hospital. I learned that until 1957 Black Americans were not allowed to swim in the Lafayette, Indiana municipal swimming pool. I also learned that a Black man could not get a haircut in Lafayette. He had to go to Indianapolis or Kokomo. If I remember correctly, it was circa 1965 that Eli Lilly & Company brought a black barber from Indianapolis to the community to solve that injustice.

I moved from the laboratory into hospital administration in 1975. The hospital had extraordinarily little parking and had started buying properties to create parking lots. One of my first administrative jobs was to find houses that would be suitable for those families, mostly black, that we were displacing. It went something like this. We would talk to the family, determine their housing needs, and then look at houses for sale that were of proper size and in good condition. The price those houses were selling for is what we offered to pay for the family's dilapidated house. The offers were eagerly accepted, and the hospital was responsible for fully integrating the black community of Lafayette.

The Second Baptist Church, built in 1865, was an integral part of the black community. We had negotiated to buy the church, but before they would consummate the sale, the congregation wanted a presentation about our plans and assurances that we would build a new Dennis Burton Day Care Center that was housed in the church. Dennis was a black man who had been raised in the neighborhood and was the first Tippecanoe County resident to die in the Vietnam War. I scheduled a time to make the presentation and walked into the church. It was then that I experienced, for a second or two, what I believe the Black Americans of the community experienced most of their lives. When I walked in there was dead silence and all eyes were trained on the only white man in the room. It was an extremely uncomfortable feeling. Within a second or two I was warmly greeted, the meeting went well, they agreed to sell us the church and we led a successful community wide campaign to raise $750,000 for a new day care center.

My wife, Betty, was raised in Chicago, and while we were dating, we experienced the Chicago race riots. We supported the Civil Rights Act of 1964 and the Voting Rights Act of 1965. I remember watching, on television, Dr. Martin Luther King, Jr.'s August 28, 1963 "I Have a Dream" speech. These words from his speech were seared in my mind and I think of them almost every day: "I have a dream that my four children will one day live in a nation where they will not be judged by the color of their skin but by the content of their character." The CEO of my hospital, Paul E. Hess, was an administrator at St. Joseph's Hospital in Memphis, Tennessee in 1968 and announced to the world that Dr. King had died. I heard many times about the details of that tragic day.

It was around 18 years ago that Betty and I were preparing to visit relatives in Chicago who had purchased a house in a predominantly black neighborhood. We were taking our Pug puppy, Phoebe, with us, and while going to our car she got away and ran across the street to a long-time neighbor standing by his pickup truck. He shood her away and as my wife was retrieving her, he said, "You better keep her out of here, she might get killed."

After arriving in Chicago, Betty was preparing to take Phoebe for a walk and Phoebe wiggled from her hands and ran toward a group of Black men standing about 50 yards away. The men corralled Phoebe and handed her to Betty, who got a leash on her and continued with the walk down the block. When Betty returned a few minutes later she was crying and visibly shaken. I asked her what had happened, and she said, "Nothing. I am just so upset that those men who had never seen me were so much nicer to me than my own neighbor." Blacks and Whites do not hate each other. Most people are nice, and a few are asses. Color does not matter.

I especially agree with Dr. Ben Carson: "We will know that America has made substantial social progress when black Americans are not expected to adhere to any particular political philosophy, just as white Americans do not have a prescribed political doctrine to which they must adhere. Fortunately, we get to choose whether we are going to use the magnificent gray matter that sits between our ears – as opposed to our skin color – to determine who we are and our course of action."[40]

I thought that through my life experiences, my reading and listening to others, that I have at least an average level of political and social awareness of racial injustices, and that in today's vernacular, I am Woke. However, I WAS WRONG! VERY WRONG!

Steve Hilton woke me up about Wokeism. Wokeism is the real enemy within. Wokeism is about thinking the worst about everything. Think the world is out to get you. Think victimhood is sainthood. It says thou shall not think for yourself or hold an opposing view.[41] Wokeism is not new. It may have come to life in a big way with the death of George Floyd, but that is not when, or where, it began.

---

[40] Dr. Ben Carson, Gray Matter, The Stuff that Really Matters, January, 2014.
[41] The Next Revolution, Hilton, Steve, Fox News, April 4, 2021.

According to Hilton, Wokeism began in Germany at the Institute for Social Research in 1923. A group of Marxist philosophers was trying to figure out why the proletariat was standing in the way of a worldwide communist revolution. They discovered that it was not economic issues that kept people from supporting communism but rather family, religion, and culture. To dismantle these building blocks, they developed "Critical Theory."

In the 1960s, Critical Theory found its way to Herbert Marcuse in Columbia University's Sociology Department. In his book, <u>The One-Dimensional Man</u>, Marcuse says the purpose of higher education must shift from studying the world to changing it. It must shift from education to activism. He presented a blueprint for social revolution and added race as a component. He believed that an alliance of racial minorities, liberal intelligentsia, and violent outside activists would take power. He introduced "Representative Tolerance" that violence by the radical left must be tolerated but never accepted by the right.

Critical Theory became Critical Race Theory and spread throughout the 70s, 80s and 90s. In 1989, Kimberly Crenshaw coined the term "Intersectionality" to describe how different parts of your identity, race, gender, and sexuality could intersect and compound your oppression.

Ayanne Hirsi Ali believes that wokeism has captured the institutions of power through: 1.) pollution of language where things are sugarcoated in wonderful sounding words like, justice and equality, 2.) pollution of emotions – an appeal to compassion for another and then using it for something sinister like segregation and the new found racism, 3.) pollution of human relations – we have been divided into many groups treated as a zero sum game – you cannot lift one group without pushing another group down.[42]

I recommend you read, <u>Cynical Theories</u>, How Activist Scholarship Made Everything about Race, Gender, and Identity – and Why This Harms Everybody. It was written by Helen Pluckrose & James Lindsay and published August 25, 2020, by Pitchstone Publishing.

Let us move on to Cancel Culture. Merriam-Webster defines Cancel Culture as: "The practice or tendency of engaging in mass canceling as a way of expressing disapproval and exerting social pressure." Cancel Culture

---

[42] Ibid.

has been around for centuries, but it was not known as Cancel Culture – it was known as ostracism. It was throwing someone out of a social circle or profession. "Ostracism was a political process used in 5th-century BCE Athens whereby those individuals considered too powerful or dangerous to the city were exiled for 10 years by popular vote. Some of the greatest names in Greek history fell victim to the process, although, as the votes were often not personal but based on policies..."[43]

Back to modern times and Cancel Culture. There are many definitions of Cancel Culture other than that provided by Merriam-Webster. Here are a couple from the online urban dictionary. "A modern internet phenomenon where a person is ejected from influence or fame by questionable actions. It is caused by a critical mass of people who are quick to judge and slow to question. It is commonly caused by an accusation, whether that accusation has merit or not. It is a direct result of the ignorance of people caused by communication technologies outpacing the growth in available knowledge of a person."[44] However, this is my favorite: "Cancel culture is just a bunch of narcissistic psychopaths on social media who vilify people to feel important. They always take the chance when given and stretch it as much as they can, as long as they can create a narrative that portrays people in a bad light, no matter the context... What they want in the end is useless (expletive deleted) prestige instead of thoughtful and considerate nourishment of people."[45]

The Chinese even have a word for Woke American Liberals – Baizuo. The literal translation is White Left. Baizuo describes people who cannot tolerate different opinions. It is used to refer to Western leftist ideologies primarily espoused by white leftists. It is a sarcastic reference to those whose political opinions are perceived as being guided by emotions or a hypocritical show of selflessness and empathy.[46]

Going back to Woke. Having political and social awareness, and professing what you believe to be true, does not immunize you against Cancel Culture. If your experiences and beliefs differ from those of the

---

[43] Ostracism, Cartwright, Mark, World History Encyclopedia, March 30, 2016.

[44] www.urbandictionary.com.

[45] https://www.urbandictionary.com/define.php?term+Cancel%Culture, March 30, 2021.

[46] en.m.wikipedia.org.

Woke progressive left, you are not Woke and you are subject to being cancelled. Cancelled for saying or writing what you believe to be true. This is happening in America – the land of the free and the home of the brave.

The combination of the Progressive Woke Culture and the Cancel Culture are two of the most anti-American phenomena to take hold of America in decades. Since abbreviations are in common use today, I will be referring to this phenomenon as WCC (Woke Cancel Culture).

WCC is an attack on the right to free speech guaranteed in the First Amendment to the Constitution. Free speech is a fundamental right that separates America from Socialist, Communist and autocratic forms of government. Today, WCC has taken the form of iron-fisted leftism. If you disagree with the approved message, you will be punished! If the progressive left decides they don't like something, it will be removed. If you speak out against the approved message, you will be censured, you may be doxed and could lose your job. WCC has entered every aspect of American's lives.

Aaron Reitz writes, "In the Marine Corps, we don't have *quotas*, but we do have *goals*. And Marines *accomplish* goals, my officer-in-charge told me and a few brand-new second lieutenants, each of us assigned to temporary recruiting duty while awaiting orders to Quantico. The captain then told us we had to sign up a certain number of college-enrolled racial minorities and females. No need to be too strict on physical fitness or academics, he said. Just bring them in. That was in 2009. Discrimination of this sort has been an ingrained yet lamentable part of the military's recruitment, retention, and promotion practices for many years. But my fellow officers and I could not have imagined that 12 years later, our disagreement with these policies would get us labeled "racist," "sexist," "bigoted" or "extremists" worthy of "eradication" and "elimination" from the USMC. Yet the Sergeant Major of the Marine Corps said as much in his February 22, "core values" memo."[47]

Reitz continues, "January 6 (when protestors stormed the Capital Building in Washington, D.C) provided the pretext that the government, media and Democratic Party needed to drum up paranoia about white-nationalist domestic terrorism. A month later, Secretary of Defense Lloyd

---

[47] From Soft Liberalism to Iron-Fisted Leftism in Today's U.S. Military, Reitz, Aaron, Newsweek, March 19, 2021.

Austin issued a memo to all Pentagon leadership laying the groundwork for my unit's Sunday morning indoctrination. In his memo, Austin announced that the Department of Defense 'will not tolerate...actions associated with extremist or dissident ideologies' and ordered all 1.4 million personnel to receive 'extremism' training."[48]

Reitz further continues, "Acting Secretary of the Navy Thomas Harker followed with his own memo. He announced the objective for the entire Navy Department: nothing short of 'eradicating extremism.' How? By rooting out 'actions that betray our oaths' like promoting 'ideology' or 'doctrine' that challenges the 'gender identity and sexual orientation' agenda or advancing efforts that allegedly 'deprive individuals of their civil rights.' In other words, advocating for the Biblical view of sex and marriage in law and policy is, according to today's armed forces, tantamount to oath betrayal."[49]

Finally, Reitz stated, "Then came the Marine Corps' turn to mouth the right things about 'extremism.' In late February, the highest-ranking enlisted Marine issued a memo to all hands condemning our institutional failure to 'completely eliminate,' 'eradicate,' and 'conquer' all 'racists, bigots, homophobes, and bullies.'"[50] According to Nick Allen, the Pentagon may reverse gender-neutral physical fitness test for US Army soldiers. "An early Pentagon study showed that women were failing the [Army Combat Fitness Test] at a rate of 65 per cent, while only 10 per cent of men did..."[51]

The U.S. military exists to serve the American people, to defend the Nation, and to protect vital national interests. I have not been able to find any official document stating that a purpose of the military is to engage in social engineering. In the words of Otto Von Bismarck: "We the unwilling. Led by the unqualified. To kill the unfortunate. Die for the ungrateful."[52] I pray this is not where our leaders are taking or have taken us.

WCC is not limited to racial issues. Senator Josh Hawley said, "If you dare to think for yourself, dare to demand the Constitution be followed

---

[48] Ibid.
[49] Ibid.
[50] Ibid.
[51] Pentagon may reverse gender-neutral physical fitness test for US Army Soldiers, Allen, Nick, The Telegraph, March 13, 2021.
[52] Pionterest.com.

or dare to question a child choosing their own gender, you will be mocked and canceled."[53] I'll add to Senator Hawley's list of progressive left subjects that should not be questioned: Multiple gender identities, defunding of the police, reparations for Black Americans, money for education should stay in public schools, teaching the 1619 project, cancelling the 2nd Amendment, and abortion rights.

Helen Lewis, in an article from The Atlantic writes, "Tumbrels are rattling through the streets of the internet. Over the past few years, online-led social movements have deposed gropers, exposed bullies – and sometimes ruined the lives of the innocent."[54] Lewis continues with," Perhaps the most egregious example of this is the random firings of individuals, some of whose infractions are minor, and some of whom are entirely innocent of any bad behavior. Niel Golightly, the communications chief at the aircraft company Boeing, stepped down over a 33-year-old article arguing that women should not serve in the military. When Barack Obama, a notably progressive president, only changed his mind on gay marriage in the 2010s, how many Americans' views from 1987 would hold up to scrutiny by today's standards?"[55]

I hear a lot about big tech companies, Facebook, Twitter, and Silicon Valley cancelling individuals and political positions they disagree with through censorship and the squelching of free speech. "In a March 27, 2021, interview, former President Donald Trump said that there's hope for a 2024 run – and Facebook almost immediately yanked video of the interview from its site, stating that the 'voice of Donald Trump' is not permitted on the social media network. Following the interview, a Facebook employee reportedly messaged several Trump affiliates and warned that any such content would be removed from the platform and that continued infractions could result in 'additional limitations on accounts that posted it.' This guidance applies to all campaign accounts

---

[53] Why Attacking 'Cancel Culture' and 'Woke' People is Becoming the GOP's New Political Strategy, Bacon, Perry Jr., March 17, 2021.
[54] How Capitalism Drives Cancel Culture, Lewis, Helen, The Atlantic, July 14, 2020.
[55] Ibid.

and Pages, including Team Trump, other campaign messaging vehicles on our platforms, and former surrogates."[56]

It is not just high-profile conservatives that are being censored, but so are every-day, average Americans expressing their opinions. On April 12, 2021, my wife shared a Facebook post by Anita Sherman of Independent Women's Voice, "If you can get arrested for hunting or fishing without a license, but not for entering and remaining in the country illegally – you might live in a nation that was founded by geniuses but is run by idiots." She then received the following message from Facebook: "We removed your post because it was true and made liberals look like liars and idiots, which is in violation of Facebook Community Standards." So, it is okay for liberals to tell lies about conservative actions but if conservatives tell the truth about liberals it violates "Facebook Community Standards." Huh? It has become clear that censorship and cancel culture is about one thing only – protecting far-left ideology!

Based on the 2020 presidential election half of the voters like Trump and the other half do not like him and many hate him. I understand the divide, but love him or hate him, he should be allowed to be heard. Amazon removed Parler, an online social media platform that mostly attracted conservatives. Amazon was opposed to the messages being shared on Parler, so it just canceled their voices. About four in every five Americans (approximately 250 million people) have profiles on social media. Big tech companies have a duty to allow differing views on their public platforms. America cannot have an informed public if conservative voices are silenced.

Big tech is not the only culprit cancelling conservative views. The media is just as bad. News stories that do not fit the progressive narrative either are not published or are given just a few lines in an obscure location. For example, there was sparse coverage of the discovery of Hunter Biden's laptop and millions of dollars he received from Russian and Ukranian oligarchs. And no, NPR, the Hunter Biden laptop story was not discredited.[57] I am willing to bet a lot of money that if that had been one of Donald Trump's children the story would have had massive coverage.

---

[56] Taylor, Sarah, Blaze Media/News, March 31, 2021.
[57] In Our Opinion, Washington Examiner, Carney, Timothy P. and Freddoso, David, April 2, 2021.

In another blatant example, CNN claims there is no way to determine gender at birth. "It's not possible to know a person's gender identity at birth, and there is no consensus criteria for assigning sex at birth," CNN political reporter Devan Cole wrote Tuesday in a story promoted as straight news and not an opinion piece."[58] Sorry Mr. Cole, biology of sex has not changed since my high school biology days – females have XX chromosomes and males have XY chromosomes and they are present at birth.

Don Purdum, an independent political analyst asks, "Where was the media during the Biden press conference? During the four years of the Trump presidency, the former president never shied away from the press or a question, even if he wanted to. It is a safe statement to make that the press was less than favorable to the former president, and at times outright hostile. They did not just dislike the man, but they also did not like his conservative policies. Now, in comes Joe Biden, the self-proclaimed moderate who is proving to be anything but as he embraces the far-left side of the Democratic Party. On Thursday, March 25, at Biden's first press conference since taking over the Oval Office, the press put on a horrid display. Journalists asked him few questions of substance, and when they did, it was to support a leftist position. Media critic for The Hill, Joe Concha, went as far as to say the press was a 'disgrace' and an 'embarrassment.'"[59]

Sally Kent said, "Tucker Carlson didn't hold back on attacking NBC's news anchor, Lester Holt's idea that journalists should not commit to 'fairness' in the name of fighting misinformation. Carlson blasted Holt's claim that given two sides 'equal weight' was outdated calling the comment 'demented.'"[60]

Gannett Co., which publishes USA TODAY, dropped the conservative comic strip "Mallard Filmore." Ken Paulson noted that, "last August, some newspapers canceled the "Six Chix" cartoon because it depicted a white

---

[58] CNN Claims There's No Way to Determine Gender at Birth in Bias-Filled Report on Trans Athletics, Chang, Samantha, The Western Journal, March 31, 2021.

[59] Where Was the Media During the Biden Press Conference/, Purdum, Don, Independent Political Analyst, AbsoluteNews, March 28, 2021.

[60] Fox News (https://www.foxnews.com/media/tucker-carlson-lester-holt-fairness), Kent, Sally, April 1, 2021.

woman who was clueless about both COVID-19 and Black Lives Matter."[61] Is this selective editing or canceling opposing views? You decide!

Corporations are getting into the act too. President Biden and the mainstream media have repeated unadulterated lies about the recently passed Georgia voting laws stating they reduce the time for voting and the requirement of identification for voting is a return to "Jim Crowe." The President encouraged Major League Baseball (MLB) to move the All-Star game and the MLB draft out of Atlanta (which they did) to protest the new law. Coca-Cola and Delta Airlines jumped on board, condemned the law, and supported the MLB action out of fear of being cancelled.

Schools get into the act too. Some of the books (that should be mandatory reading) frequently banned from school reading are: The Adventures of Huckleberry Finn, The Catcher in the Rye, The Hunger Games, Of Mice and Men, To Kill a Mockingbird, 1984, and Brave New World. School curricula are being infused with social engineering. The 1619 Project, discussed in Chapter Three, teaches Black Americans to hate White Americans.

Ashe Schow reports that, "The Oregon Department of Education is now promoting a program for teachers that seeks to 'disman[tle] racism in mathematics,' alleging that focusing on finding the right answer is a symbol of white supremacy."[62] Based on standardized test scores I have seen lately (more on that in subsequent chapters), our schools should forget social engineering and look back to 1907 and sing Will Cobb's song, "School days, school days, dear old golden rule days, readin' and 'ritin' and 'rithmetic' taught to the tune of the hickory stick."

I now know for sure that I AM NOT WOKE! I do not want to be Woke! I will never be Woke! There is no way I can ever support a movement designed to break down family and destroy religion and our culture!

---

[61] Paulson, Ken, Director of the Free Speech Center at Middle Tennessee State University.

[62] Oregon Promotes Program Focused On 'Dismantling Racism in Mathematics,' Says Finding The Right Answer a Sign of White Supremacy, Schow, Ashe, The Daily Wire, February 13, 2021.

ACTIONS

1. Question Everything! That includes everything I write about in this book. Do your own research and decide what you believe to be the truth.
2. Do not politicize everything.
3. The Georgia legislature eliminated the financial incentives they provide to Delta Airlines – more states should do the same to Woke compliant companies they subsidize.
4. Cities and states should stop subsidizing woke compliant professional athletic teams and facilities.
5. Do not make racism the root of all problems.
6. As Ben Carson said (paraphrased), choose to use the magnificent gray matter that sits between your ears – as opposed to our skin color – to determine who you are and your course of action.
7. Keep a watchful eye on what is being taught in your schools.
8. Hold politicians accountable.
9. Hold the media accountable.
10. Hold yourself accountable.

CHAPTER SIX

Immigration

Let us get the boring stuff out of the way. The Immigration and Nationality Act (INA) was enacted in 1952. It collected the many provisions and reorganized the structure of immigration law. The INA has been amended many times and contains many of the most important provisions of immigration law. If you want the details of all the legislation over the years you should go to the U.S. Citizenship and Immigration Services website.

The American Immigration Council published a fact sheet entitled, "How the United States Immigration System Works."[63] It is a nice summary of immigration law today and I will quote some elements of the fact sheet:

- The INA allows up to 675,000 permanent immigrant visas each year.
- There are no limits on the annual admission of U.S. citizens' spouses, parents, and children under the age of 21.
- Each year, the president is required to consult with Congress and set an annual number of refugees to be admitted through the Refugee Resettlement Process.
- The refugee ceiling in 2017 was 110,000 and dropped to 45,000 in 2018 and to 30,000 in 2019. The cap was set to 18,000 on September 26, 2019.

---

[63] How the United States Immigration System Works, American Immigration Council, October 10, 2019.

- Once a person obtains an immigrant visa and comes to the United States, they become a lawful permanent resident (LPR) and are permitted to work and live lawfully and permanently in the United States.
- After living in the United States for five years (sometimes three), LPRs are eligible to apply for U.S. citizenship.
- It is impossible to apply for citizenship through the normal process without first becoming an LPR.
- U.S. citizens and LPRs are allowed to bring certain family members to the United States.
- Family-based immigrants are not to exceed 480,000.
- In Fiscal Year 2017, family-based immigrants comprised 66 percent of all new LPRs.
- Temporary employment-based visa classifications permit employers to hire and petition for foreign nationals for specific jobs for limited periods. There are more than 20 types of visas for temporary nonimmigrant workers.
- The limit for permanent employment-based immigrants is 140,000 per year.
- Currently, no group of permanent immigrants from a single country can exceed seven percent of the total number immigrating to the United States in a single fiscal year.
- There are several categories of legal admission available to people who are fleeing persecution or are unable to return to their homeland due to life-threatening or extraordinary conditions.
- Asylum is available to persons already in the United States who are seeking protection. There is no limit on the number who may be granted asylum. 26,568 individuals were granted asylum in fiscal year 2017.
- Temporary Protected Status (TPS) is granted to people who are in the United States but cannot return to their home country because of natural disaster, extraordinary temporary conditions, or ongoing armed conflict. TPS is granted for 6, 12 or 18 months but may be extended.
- Deferred Action for Childhood Arrivals (DACA) was established in 2012. It permits children under the age of 16 who had resided

continuously in the United States since June 15, 2007, to remain in the United States to work lawfully for at least two years. It does not confer any path to permanent legal status and requires renewal every two years.

Okay, enough of what our elected officials have done. Now let us get to what they have not done and how immigration has become strictly a political animal. Most importantly, IMMIGRATION IS A PRIVILEGE, NOT A RIGHT! People do not have the right to just come in and say, "I'm here to stay." You do not just allow people to walk into your home and announce that they will be staying. Most of us would politely ask them to leave and if they did not, we would call the police (if there are any left after the "defund the police movement") and have them escorted out. The door to your home is the "border" between you and the outside world.

President Ronald Reagan is credited with saying, "A nation that cannot control its borders is not a nation." Thomas Jefferson is credited with saying, "A country with no Border is not a country." Since I could not find documentation to prove those quotes, I am going to say them: 1.) A nation that cannot control its borders is not a nation and, 2.) A country with no Border is not a country. There they are. If you need to quote them and cannot find credible references, you can quote me. They are both true. A home is not a home without walls and a door. A city is not a city without city limits. A county is not a county without county lines. A state is not a state without state lines and a country is not a country without borders. Argue about it if you like, but if you want to win the argument with me, you will need proof, not just opinion.

I need to make it clear that I AM NOT anti-immigration. I know that we need to invite people in to meet the needs of the country. We may need farm workers in some parts of the country. We may need highly skilled workers in some industries. We may need some doctors or other professionals but there are also some that we do not need more of – lawyers for example. I am for LEGAL immigration based on the needs of the country and merit.

The Statue of Liberty has watched over New York Harbor since 1886 and is inscribed with these words written by Emma Lazarus in 1883: "Give me your tired, your poor, Your huddled masses yearning to breathe free,

The wretched refuse of your teeming shore. Send these, the homeless, tempest-tost to me, I lift my lamp beside the golden door!" "The golden door is a beacon of promise beckoning immigrants to embrace a new land and all it offers. Another meaning of the golden door is that anything worthwhile is worth fighting and working hard for, and gold is emblematic of something worthwhile."[64] Lazarus wrote the poem in 1883 to raise money for the construction of the pedestal for the Statue of Liberty.

Is a fund-raising poem an open invitation to everyone in the world to enter the United States at will? I do not think so and I believe having immigration laws support my belief.

Ellis Island is further support for my belief that Lazarus' words are not an open invitation. Ellis Island was an immigrant inspection station in the United States from 1892 to 1954 and processed nearly 12 million immigrants under federal law. About two percent were determined to be unfit to enter. Those showing any signs of contagious disease, poor physique, feeblemindedness or insanity could be turned away on the grounds that they were likely to become a ward of the state.

In the late 1880s, after the Civil War, where citizens were fighting against citizens, the country was focused on reconstruction of the country. Business was increasing, work was plentiful, and the country was growing. The government decided to allow any immigrants into the country and provide them with the opportunity to be part of the growth.

The country was not wide open to immigrants until after the Civil War when the country was growing and needed workers. The death of 620,000 men in the Civil War contributed to the need for workers. The golden door was a promise beckoning immigrants to embrace a new land and all it offers. Embracing all it offers is an extremely important concept. It means embrace America and all that it means – freedom, liberty, and opportunity for all who are willing to work hard for it.

We have a system for legal immigration, but it is not perfect - more about that later. What is important to focus on now is the illegal immigration we are experiencing at our southern border today. I will not be politically correct. If someone enters the country illegally, they are illegal aliens, not undocumented residents. I hear the cries that no human is illegal, and I am not calling people illegal – I am calling their entry into our country illegal.

---

[64] https://www.enotes.com,what-does-golden-door-mean.

Despite what some in Washington, D.C. and the media say, we do have a major crisis on our hands. It is a humanitarian crisis, an economic crisis, and a political crisis. However, this is not a crisis like Hurricane Katrina – a natural disaster. The border crisis is the result of political decisions – a manmade crisis.

Illegal immigration has been a recurring issue for decades, contributed to by both political parties. The politicians of both parties have failed to work together to tackle immigration reform legislation. Congressional representatives are pressured from all sides. The liberal elites want unbridled immigration to keep the supply of labor high which leads to lower pay for workers. The conservatives want controlled immigration to protect the economy and the American workers. We have immigration laws, but they are not enforced, sometimes at the federal level and at other times at the state and local levels. Today, we do not have border enforcement and we have sanctuary cities and states.

President Trump experienced a surge at the southern border, as most presidents have in the spring months, and he took action to stem the flow. He nearly finished a wall, ended the catch-and-release policy (where illegal aliens were caught and immediately released into America), started the stay-in-Mexico policy, and made bilateral agreements with Guatemala, El Salvadore, and Honduras to help slow the flow of immigrants seeking asylum. Many thought these, along with other of his immigration policies, if not illegal were certainly wrong and even cruel and inhumane. I am not going to take those issues on here but do want to acknowledge they exist. What I do know is that his southern border policies were working during the last months of his presidency and illegal immigration was trending to a 45-year low.

Anyone who was even semi-conscious during the 2020 presidential campaign knew that President Trump and candidate Biden did not have much respect for each other and that they disagreed on about every issue. Whether driven by strong policy differences or sheer hatred for Trump, immediately upon taking office, President Biden reversed all of Trump's southern border policies. Construction on the wall was halted, catch-and-release was reinstated, stay-in-Mexico was rescinded, and a 100-day moratorium placed on deportations. These actions were interpreted, rightly or wrongly, by Central America residents as an invitation to come to America.

Now we have a mess. It is so bad that the Biden administration is denying the press access to the detention and processing centers and will not allow the press to interview Custom and Border Patrol (CBP) officers or accompany them (ride-along) on their patrols. So much for transparency!

Reports, from anonymous CBP staff and Senators who visited the border in late March, are that in Donna, TX holding facility designed for 250 people is housing 4,000 – that is 1,600 percent of capacity. The Epoch Times reports (from an anonymous CBP agent), "As many as 80 people are squeezed into each 24 by 30-foot cell. The detainees are often laying on top of each other because there is no room to sleep. The family-unit holding cells smell like urine and vomit. Fights break out in the unaccompanied-minor cells. Scabies, lice, the flu, and Covid-19 run rampant. One or two agents are left to control 300 to 500 people during a shift."[65] Now we are hearing reports about the rape of minors in the holding facilities. We are on pace to have more than 1,000,000 illegal border crossings this year – a 20-year high. That excludes the "got-aways" (those who cross without being caught) and those could double that number.

I do not understand how the Biden administration can allow this to continue. In about 1990, I was serving on the board of directors for Tippecanoe County Child Care (TCCC). TCCC had a couple of childcare centers and sponsored several childcare homes in two or three surrounding counties – private homes where childcare was provided. I remember a case in which a county child and protective services department had revoked the license of a childcare home. The woman had been providing childcare for ten years or more and had excellent reviews from the children's parents. We learned that her license had been revoked because of child abuse. A complaint had been filed by a neighbor who observed what she believed to be child abuse. The "abuse" occurred in a wading pool where two children about age 4 or so were playing with supervision. One child pulled down the swimming trunks of the other child. That was the child abuse that resulted in a license revocation and try as we may, we were unable to get her license renewed. If that is child abuse, I cannot find words to describe what is happening on our border.

---

[65] Cuthbertson, Charlotte, The Epoch Times, Fox News, Hannity, March 24, 2021.

On March 30, 2021, CBP had 18,000 children in custody. The "low-end" estimate from CBP is that 184,000 migrant children will cross the border this fiscal year, many of which are unaccompanied. That number does not include an estimate for the "got-aways" and that number could be one or more for each one caught. I just saw a video on Fox News two days ago showing a human trafficker dropping two little girls (ages 3 and 5) over a 14' wall and then running back into Mexico. When the cartels draw CBP to an area by flooding it with illegals, that opens other areas for their drug smuggling. These cartels are evil!

According to Tom Homan, former director of Immigration and Customs Enforcement (ICE), 50 percent or more of those making the perilous journey to the southern border are abused and about 25 percent of women and young girls are raped. The cost to be taken across the border ranges from $3,000 to $5,000 for those coming from Central America while those coming from foreign countries are charged $10,000 and more. Those who do not have all the money to pay the human traffickers are held in servitude or child slavery and women and girls sold into the sex trade. Homan further states that groups of 8 – 10 adults claiming to be family and accompanied by a child are released into the country often On Their Own Recognizance (OTR). These people are automatically qualified to work. They then compete with American citizens for the low-skilled work. If a court date is given for an asylum hearing it may be 4-5 years in the future and, according to Homan, about 90 percent of the asylum claims are bogus.

Once in the country, you and I pay the bills – the cost of sending them throughout the country along with housing, education, and health care all add up. $86 million has been allocated to pay for hotel rooms for illegal immigrants and in San Diego immigrant children were receiving in-person education while 130,000 students in the San Diego school district are in virtual classrooms. According to Kenneth Wolfe, a spokesman for HHS's Administration for Children and Families, "Before they (illegal immigrant minors) are released to a family member or a sponsor in the U.S., the unaccompanied minors spend an average of 31 days in HHS custody."[66] He further stated the average daily cost per minor is "approximately $775

---

[66] https://www.newsmax.com/t/newsmax/article/1016967?ns_mail_...60-million-portman&year=2021&month=04&date-9&id=1016967.

per day based on past experience."[67] $775 per day times 31 days equals $24,025 for each minor at temporary facilities.

An alleged coyote said to Ryan Saavedra of Univision: "Biden's 'benefits' gave migrants 'the courage' to illegally enter U.S." Another said he is making a very good living bringing people across the border. Customs and Border Protection officials told FOX News that the smuggling revenue in February averaged $14.6 million per day. The president of Mexico is now calling Biden the migrant president. President Biden has placed Vice President Harris in charge of the border crisis. There is no prospect for improvement since neither President Biden nor Vice President Harris have visited the border as of today, June 22, 2021. Besides, mass illegal immigration fits their political narrative.

We have more than 500,000 homeless (40,000 are veterans) and 48.8 million Americans, including 16.2 million children, live in households that lack the means to get enough nutritious food on a regular basis. You and I are chastised if we don't wear a mask during the Covid pandemic, but illegal aliens are released into the country without even being tested for Covid. The elite will not to refer to what is happening on the border as a crisis. To them, it is not a crisis. It is an orchestrated plan to flood the country with more people that are dependent on the government and will vote to keep them in power. Be assured, If HR1/S1 passes, they will soon be voters. There will be a path to citizenship (and all the associated benefits) for most, if not all, who can make it to America. The sole purpose of the unabated flow of illegal immigration is to change the demographics of America, neutralize the vote of current American citizens and ensure liberal control in perpetuity. This abuse of America must stop! Half of the country did not like President Trump's "America First" policies, but I and 75,000,000 others sure do not like the current "America Last" policies.

---

[67] Ibid.

ACTIONS

1. To stem the flow of illegals now, finish the wall, reinstate stay-in-Mexico, and stop catch and release.
2. Demand that the immigration laws in effect now be enforced.
3. Demand that your elected officials work together to create a well-functioning immigration system that is responsive to America's needs.
4. Provide a pathway to citizenship for DACA children.
5. Other than DACA children, no one who enters the country illegally should have a pathway to citizenship. Those who have lived here 15 years or more may stay but not attain citizenship.
6. Demand that the new immigration laws be enforced.
7. Hold your elected officials accountable.

CHAPTER SEVEN

Coronavirus Disease 2019

On February 11, 2020, the World Health Organization (WHO) announced the official name for the disease causing the 2019 pandemic - coronavirus disease 2019 and abbreviated COVID-19. The 'CO' is for corona, 'VI' is for virus, and 'D' is for disease.

COVID-19 is a highly infectious global pandemic. According to WebMD, "an epidemic is a disease that affects a large number of people within a community, population, or region. A pandemic is an epidemic that has spread to multiple countries or continents across the world. A simple way to remember the difference is to think of the P in pandemic as a passport to travel. So, in a way, a pandemic is a globe-trotting epidemic."

I will only have brief comments about the origin of COVID-19. As of this writing, there is no definitive proof regarding the origin of COVID-19. However, there is ample circumstantial evidence that it was the result of an accident that occurred in Wuhan, China virology laboratory.

The Wuhan Institute of Virology was conducting gain-of-function (GOF) research funded in part by Dr. Anthony Fauci, the director of the U.S. National Institute of Allergy and Infectious Disease.[68] Gain-of-function research involves experiments aimed at increasing the virulence and/or transmissibility of pathogens, especially viruses. In October 2014, the Obama White House declared a moratorium on 'monster-germ'

---

[68] Why US outsourced bat virus research to Wuhan, Lin, Dr. Christina, ISPSW Strategy Series: Focus on Defense and International Security, Issue No. 689, April 2020.

research. This included research on gain-of-function research to weaponize viruses, Middle East respiratory syndrome (MERS), and severe acute respiratory syndrome (SARS). In 2015, a U.S. National Institute of Health (NIH)-funded $3.7 million project was approved by Dr. Anthony Fauci and outsourced to China's Wuhan Institute of Virology.[69]

When COVID-19 was first discovered in Wuhan, the Chinese government forbid Chinese people from traveling to Wuhan and people from Wuhan from traveling to other parts of China. However, people from Wuhan could travel to other parts of the world. The release of the virus from the lab was probably an accident, but China did not make any effort to contain it from infecting the rest of the world and has not cooperated with worldwide efforts to confirm the source. We will never know for sure, but China may have taken advantage of an accident to weaken the world that it strives to dominate. As Rahm Emanuel said, "You never let a crisis go to waste. And what I mean by that it's an opportunity to do things you think you could not do before."[70]

On April 14, 2021, The New York Times reports 31.4 million cases and 563,987 deaths in the U.S. from COVID-19. We have known since early in the pandemic that the vulnerability to death from COVID-19 is more than a thousand-fold higher in the old and infirm than the young. For children, COVID-19 is less dangerous than many other harms, including influenza.[71] We also know that as immunity builds in the population, the risk of infection to all falls and that all populations will eventually reach herd immunity.[72]

Viruses need the cells of other organisms to survive and reproduce because they cannot capture or store energy. Viruses just do what viruses do – they hop into a cell, produce more viruses, and then go "looking" for another cell and repeat the process. Some viruses, like herpes and HIV, take up residence in the body and stick around until the host (the body) dies, but most do not. When invaded by a virus, our bodies' immune system fights back and kicks them out. While fighting the viruses, the

---

[69] Ibid.

[70] www.brainyquote.com.

[71] https://gbdeclaration.org/, Kulldorff, Dr. Martin, Gupta, Dr. Sunetra, Bhattacharya, Dr. Jay, Great Barrington Declaration, October 4, 2020.

[72] Ibid.

body tries to protect itself from further invasion and develops antibodies to stop the virus from re-infecting (immunity). Immunity can be achieved from being infected or through a vaccine. When enough people have achieved immunity for the infection rate in the population to stabilize, herd immunity has been reached. Herd immunity does not mean that there will not be any more infections. It just means the virus has a harder time finding a person who has not been infected so the rate of infection stabilizes. This means that the infection rate has become flat and is no longer increasing.

The debates about how the pandemic has been handled will go on for a long time. Some of the debates will be political, some scientific, some a combination of politics and filtered science. Each person will have to decide for themself what to believe. Today, half of the country believed it was poorly handled by President Trump and half believed he did a good job, hence, the outcome of the 2020 presidential election.

Many say there was a lack of transparency in the Trump administration despite his holding COVID-19 press briefings nearly every day for months. These briefings included his advisors Dr. Anthony Fauci and Dr. Deborah L. Birx. He was highly criticized for his federalist approach of allowing the states to manage the pandemic (with NIH and CDC providing guidelines) rather than mandating specific actions nationwide. He was criticized for not mandating a nationwide shutdown. He was criticized for not following the ever-evolving science on things like masks, social distancing, and treatments. However, I thought President Trump's message was clear – protect the vulnerable, open schools for kids, and open businesses with appropriate protections.

There are some actions that former President Trump took that were indisputably right. He halted air flights from China and Europe against the advice of Dr. Fauci. He understood that one size fits all government dictates do not work. Trump put Vice President Pence in charge of working with the states and government agencies and provided hospital ships and other facilities for the treatment of patients. He invoked the Defense Production Act to produce more personal protective equipment (PPE) and ventilators. Most of all, he implemented Operation Warp Speed that produced vaccines in record time – a few months and ordered 550 million doses before the vaccines were even approved. When the Operation was announced, Dr. Fauci said a vaccine in less than 2 years or more would be impossible. I am sure glad the president did not follow Dr. Fauci's thinking on that one. Many people do not like (read "hate") former President Trump, but he deserves credit for the things he got right.

The "Great Barrington Declaration" is a group of disease epidemiologists and public health scientists with concerns about the damaging physical and mental health impacts of the prevailing COVID-19 policies. It has the signatures of 781,613 concerned citizens (including mine), 14,021 medical and public health scientists, and 42,650 medical practitioners. This group believes that "the most compassionate approach that balances the risks and benefits of reaching herd immunity, is to allow those who are at minimal risk of death to live their lives normally to build up immunity to the virus through natural infection, while better protecting those who are at highest risk. We call this Focused Protection."[73]

"Those who are not vulnerable should immediately be allowed to resume life as normal. Simple hygiene measures, such as hand washing and staying home when sick should be practiced by everyone. Schools and universities should be open for in-person teaching. Extracurricular activities, such as sports, should be resumed. Young low-risk adults should work normally, rather than from home. Restaurants and other businesses should open. Arts, music, sports, and other cultural activities should resume. People who are more at risk may participate if they wish, while society as a whole enjoys the protection conferred upon the vulnerable by those who have built up herd immunity."[74]

President Trump and Governor Ron DeSantis of Florida got it right. Contrasting the Florida approach to that of New York Governor Andrew Cuomo reinforces the Focused Protection approach. Governor Cuomo instituted strict lockdowns, crushed businesses, and jobs, and took residents' freedoms away. DeSantis took the Focused Protection approach and the state's businesses, economy, and residents have fared quite well compared to other states with forced lockdowns. Partisans on both sides of the lockdown-no lockdown argument will not have any problem pointing to data that supports their position. You will have to choose what position to believe.

---

[73] Ibid.

[74] Ibid.

Stanford University's infectious disease scientists and epidemiologists Benavid, Oh, Bhattacharya, and Ionnides have shown that "the mitigating impact of the extraordinary measures used in almost every state was small at best – and usually harmful."[75] In President Biden's January 22, 2021, speech to the nation he said," There is nothing we can do to change the trajectory of the pandemic in the next several months." Remember, viruses do what viruses do!

There is still pressure from the left to maintain restrictions on us. It seems that those in power do not want Americans to live free. "Sadly, just as in Galileo's time, the root of our problem lies in "the experts" and vested academic interests."[76] Put simply, the "experts" made the cure worse than the disease.

One major debate about COVID-19 is over the wearing of masks. Oxford epidemiologist Sunetra Gupta says "there is no need for masks unless one is elderly or high risk."[77] Stanford's Jay Bhattacharhya has said "mask mandates are not supported by the scientific data."[78] The World Health Organization's advice of masks in the context of COVID-19 has included the following statement: "At present, there is no direct evidence (from studies on COVID-19 and in healthy people in the community) on the effectiveness of universal masking of healthy people in the community to prevent infection with respiratory viruses, including COVID-19"[79]

I see people driving alone in a car and wearing a mask. I see people walking or jogging outside with no one anywhere near, wearing a mask. I do not understand why – is it fear, a lack of common sense, or plain ignorance? I wear a mask when asked to, not because I think it does much good, but because I know many people are scared and I do not want to exacerbate their fear. However, if you wear one, for crying out loud wear it right. Cover both your nose and mouth, do not touch it all the time, do not pull it down when no one is looking, and clean or change it frequently. If you do not wear it right, you may as well not wear it.

---

[75] Science, Politics, and COVID: Will Truth Prevail?, Atlas, Scott W., Hoover Institution, Imprims, Volume 50, Number 2, February 2021.

[76] Ibid.

[77] Ibid.

[78] Ibid.

[79] Ibid.

I do have some questions for Dr. Fauci, President Biden, and Vice President Harris: Do you believe the science about the COVID-19 vaccines? Clinical trials showed the "Pfizer-BioNTech vaccine to be up to 95% effective, Moderna to be 86% effective and Johnson & Johnson 86% against severe disease in the U.S."[80] If having immunity, either naturally from having the disease or through vaccination, protects you from getting infected, and therefore prevents you from spreading it, why do we have to continue wearing masks? All three of you have been vaccinated but are always wearing masks when outside and when socially distanced – Dr. Fauci even wears two. You are giving the country mixed signals. You either believe the science that the vaccines work, or you do not. You are lying to us about either the efficacy of the vaccine or the need to wear masks – which is it?

During an April 14, 2021, congressional hearing on COVID-19, Representative Jim Jordan asked Dr. Fauci "What metrics, what measures, what has to happen before Americans get more freedoms?"[81] Dr. Fauci responded with, "when the level of infection is low enough."[82] In other settings I have heard Dr. Fauci imply it will depend on when we get enough people vaccinated. His reluctance to answer questions with specificity leads me to believe the only number of infections that will satisfy him is zero and the only way to get to zero is to stop breathing. Here are some more questions for Dr. Fauci. Do people who have had the disease need to be vaccinated? Would testing COVID-19 patients for their immune response before vaccinating them make more vaccine available to those who have not been vaccinated?

There is not any question that social distancing can help mitigate the transmission of disease. Common sense tells most sensible people that if everyone stayed in their homes and never interacted with other people there would not be much transmission of disease. Obviously, that is an unrealistic, extreme example. The question really is about how far the social distancing should be? Is it 20 feet, 10 feet, 6 feet, 3 feet, etc.?

---

[80] Comparing the COVID-19 Vaccines: How Are They Different, Katella, Kathy, Yale Medicine, April 13, 2021

[81] Dr. Fauci and the 'Liberty Thing,' Freeman, James, Wall Street Journal, April 15, 2021.

[82] Ibid.

In the late 1800s, German scientist Carl Flugge had a hunch: "Maybe if you maintain enough physical distance between people who are sick and those who are well, you can prevent the spread of pathogens from person to person."[83] In a picture taken by Professor Marshall Jennison from MIT and published in a research paper, we got one of the first images of a man in the act of sneezing. Jennison maintains that "Back then, scientists maintained that most of the infectious gunk people expel (say, about 90% of their pathogens) travel less than 6 feet away."[84] That is where the 6-foot guideline came from.

The World Health Organization was recommending a 3-foot spacing. This recommendation goes back to work done in the 1930s by Harvard researcher William Wells who studied tuberculosis. He found "that droplets – bits of spit, mucus, and sputum emitted when we breath, cough or sneeze tend to land within three feet of where they're expelled.[85] That's where the 3-foot guideline came from.

I do not know what distance is right. What I do know is that I am going live as normal of a life as possible, I will be with my family whenever possible, and I am going to hug them! Others must feel the same. We recently attended a funeral and no one either wore a mask or social distanced and we have not heard any reports that it was a super-spreader event. Thankfully, there are some people who believe in returning to a pre-COVID-19 normalcy even though our elite leaders do not want it to happen.

The goal of the fight against COVID-19 should not be to prevent people from getting the virus. People getting the virus and getting vaccinated lead to herd immunity. The goal should be to minimize the deaths of those who do contract the disease. Unfortunately, New York Governor Andrew Cuomo, did not understand that when he ordered COVID-19 positive patients to be sent back into nursing homes where thousands died because of his irresponsible actions.

There are things in addition to vaccinations, social distancing, and masks that we can do to minimize deaths from COVID-19. Data from the

---

[83] Businessinsider.com, April 14, 2021.

[84] Ibid.

[85] From Our Obsession, Foley, Katherine Ellen, Health and Science reporter, Quartz, April 15, 2020.

World Obesity Federation found "a dramatic correlation between countries' death and obesity rates, shedding new light on the role obesity has played in driving a global death toll of over 2.5 million."[86] The following are paraphrased findings from that report:

- 2.2 million of the pandemic's 2.5 million global deaths were in countries with high levels of obesity.
- Death rates were 10X higher in countries where more than 50% of the population is overweight.
- The U.K. has the third-highest death rate (184 per 100,000 population) with 63.7% of adults classified as overweight. The U.S. death rate is 152.49 per 100,000 population and 67.9% living with obesity.
- Vietnam's death rate of 0.04 per 100,000 is the lowest in the world and reports an adult obesity rate of 18.3%.
- There is not a single example internationally if a country with low levels of obesity (less than 40%) and high death rates.

Our own CDC has warned that having obesity may triple the risk of hospitalization due to COVID-19 infection. To dig deeper into the obesity problem in the U.S. I suggest you read the book, <u>Hooked: Food, Free Will, and How the Food Giants Exploit Our Addictions</u>, by Michael Moss. Moss exposes how the processed food industry exploits our evolutionary instincts, the emotions we associate with food, and legal loopholes in their pursuit of profit over public health.

The government is considering even more restrictions on us now with what they are calling a Vaccine Passport. Now they want to track us. It is under the guise of controlling the spread of COVID-19. What they are trying to push is that you do not need a picture ID to vote, however you need a Vaccine Passport to use public transportation, go to sporting events, go to movie theaters, enter restaurants, etc. I wonder, how does a person who has recovered from COVID-19 and does not get vaccinated, get a Vaccine Passport?

---

[86] Obesity And Covid Death Rate Closely Linked In New Study, McEvoy, Jemima, Forbes, March 4, 2021.

At this writing I do not have enough information on the various vaccine passport proposals to comment about specific details, but I do have what my gut tells me – vaccine passports would open the door for the government to track you everywhere you go, everything you do, everyone you contact, and even have access to your health records. This sounds like Communist China to me.

ACTIONS

1. Take care of the most vulnerable – those over 65, those with comorbidities like diabetes, lung disease, obesity, etc.
2. If you are among the most vulnerable, take care of yourself. Limit your social contacts until you get vaccinated.
3. Try not to be afraid – use common sense hygiene rules like washing your hands regularly.
4. Live as normal of life as possible – see friends, go to work, participate in social activities.
5. Listen to your doctor, but also educate yourself.
6. Get vaccinated – it will not guarantee that you will not get infected and die, but it sure reduces your chances. It is like wearing a seatbelt in your car.
7. Do not participate in making the cure worse than the disease.
8. Do not buy into the political rhetoric – much of it is driven by the desire to obtain campaign contributions and get re-elected.
9. Always remember, you are free to make your own decisions, not the government. The government works for you – stand-up and take control of your life.
10. Tell your governor and state elected officials to pass a bill barring COVID-19 "passports." This will show Big Tech we will not accept their efforts to "blackmail" us for more of our personal information.

CHAPTER EIGHT

Propaganda

Merriam-Webster defines propaganda as ideas, facts, or allegations spread deliberately to further one's cause or to damage an opposing cause. Propaganda is a battle for peoples' minds and has been around for centuries.

According to the American Historical Association (AHA) "the term 'propaganda' apparently first came into use in Europe because of the missionary activities of the Catholic church. In 1622 Pope Gregory XV created in Rome the Congregation for the Propagation of Faith. This is a commission of cardinals charged with spreading the faith and regulating church affairs in heathen lands. A College of Propaganda was set up under Pope Urban VIII to train priests for the missions."[87] Propaganda can be used to promote positive positions like peace and international good will. The AHA states that "Hitler, Mussolini, and Tojo preferred to seize upon the system for selfish ends and inhumane purposes."[88]

In our modern society we encounter propaganda everywhere–newspapers, television, the movie screen, billboards, and product advertisements. Propaganda has become an indispensable part of politics and political campaigns. It is the political propaganda I am focused on today because it influences voters and can lead to the destruction of a free society in America.

---

[87] The Story of Propaganda, American Historical Association, EM2: What is Propaganda (1944).
[88] Ibid.

Propaganda takes many forms and here are some of them paraphrased from everydayknow.com:[89]

- Name Calling – This technique tends to be quite negative, and its goal is to paint an opponent in a bad light. Presidential candidate Donald Trump was a master of it, calling opponents "Crooked Hillary" and "low-energy Jeb." During the Trump-Biden presidential debate, Joe Biden called Trump a clown and a racist.

- Glittering Generalities – This technique focuses on the positive and uses words to make something sound even better than it is. This is frequently used in "selling" legislative proposals like tax hikes, and deficit spending.

- Plain Folks – The goal of this type of propaganda is to make you think that a certain belief is what the common man believes. Today, organizations like Black Lives Matter (BLM) and Antifa, along with some elite left-wing politicians, are working hard to make people believe that police are bad and need to be defunded. Despite about 80% of the people wanting more policing, the propaganda is making headway.

- Bandwagon – The goal here uses "herd mentality" to make people feel like they are going to be left out if they do not vote a certain way, feel a certain way, or do something. This is used in advertising to make people feel like part of the crowd just by doing what 'everyone' else is doing. It is also used heavily during political election cycles in the form of voter polls – for example, if a candidate is reportedly leading by 15%, I do not need to vote because my vote will not make a difference.

- Transfer – This is when you transfer a negative connotation from one person or idea to another. This happens all the time in politics. Whatever goes wrong is always because "my predecessor" or "the other party" did it. Politicians never take responsibility for any of their mistakes.

- Card Stacking – This involves leaving out certain facts and painting an idea in the most positive light possible. No-fat products are

---

[89] Examples of Propaganda, Pococh, Courtney, everydayknow.com, May 14, 2018.

advertised as being healthy because they have little or no fat. They never mention they replace the fat with considerable amounts of sugar to make them good. The advertised low introductory rates and prices for credit cards and dietary supplements hide the scary details in exceedingly small print. Same in politics – sold as an infrastructure bill, only 27% of the proposed $2.31 trillion package goes to roads, bridges, airports, and harbors.

- Testimonials – You see this every day. Celebrities testifying about the benefits of a product. Doctors and scientists telling you how great a pharmaceutical or supplement is. It is the same when politicians use "expert" witnesses.

Now let us examine the very destructive propaganda happening right now. On Tuesday, April 14, 2021, The Sun reported, "A CNN staffer has been caught in a Tinder honeytrap sting admitting the network had a "propaganda" drive to oust Donald Trump."[90] Charlie Chester, CNN Technical Director was videoed saying, "I am 100 per cent going to say it. And I 100 per cent believe it that if it were not for CNN, I do not know that Trump would have been voted out."[91] Chester continued, "We brought in so many medical people to tell a story that was all speculation – that he was neurologically damaged, and he was losing it."[92]

CNN professes to be a news network. After this, can CNN be trusted to report the news accurately and unbiasedly? I certainly do not think so! It is the same for CBSs "60 Minutes." I used to watch "60 Minutes" regularly until I watched some programs about subjects that I was knowledgeable about. Most of those involved health care issues and I found the reports to be highly biased. I still watch it occasionally but I always fact-check it before I consider the reports to be credible.

The mainstream media is fueling the COVID-19 fear by carrying the water for Dr. Fauci's insistence that masks continue to be worn following vaccination without presenting all the facts. Breakthrough infections do

---

[90] A CNN staffer has been caught in a Tinder honeytrap sting admitting the network had a "propaganda" drive to oust Donald Trum, Knox, Patricia, The Sun, April 14, 2021.

[91] Ibid.

[92] Ibid.

occur. Those are infections that people get who have been vaccinated. Karen Weintraub reports that according to the CDC there have been 5,800 breakthrough infections out of 75,000,000 who have been fully vaccinated.[93] That means that 0.008% of those who have been vaccinated will be reinfected. Weintraub continues to say that of those 5,800, 7% were hospitalized and 1% died. In other words, your chances of being hospitalized for COVID-19 after being vaccinated is 0.0000093% and chances of dying is 0.0000013%. To put that in perspective, the odds of being struck by lightning is about 0.0065%, the odds of dying in a car accident is about 0.0107%, and the odds of being killed by a blunt object, like a hammer or club, is 0.00016%. You have a greater chance of dying from any of those than of dying from COVID-19 after you have been vaccinated. Creating excessive fear in people without presenting all the facts is propaganda.

Another of today's topics surrounds the new Georgia voting laws. President Biden and the Democrats says the new law restricts voting in future elections. President Biden says, "It's sick. Deciding that you're going to end voting at five o'clock when working people are just getting off work."[94] That is a lie – the law allows voting anywhere between 7am and 7pm. Maybe his staff did not read the new law and misinformed him, or he forgot the facts. Neither option bodes well for his honesty and accuracy. Since he repeated the statement after having time to correct it, I believe it was intentional.

There are other elements of the law that the Democrats object to, but possible the most egregious comment from the President is that the new Georgia law imposes sweeping new voting restrictions, calling it "un-American" and "Jim Crow in the 21st century."[95] The concern is that the law requires voter ID and that will restrict African Americans from voting.

My first thought about that position is that it is an extreme insult to African Americans. It says they are not capable of getting an ID. As

[93] Breakthrough Infections Occur, Weintraub, Karen, USA Today, April 19, 2021.

[94] Georgia voting: Fact-checking claims about the new election law, Horton, Jake, BBC Reality Check, April 7, 2021.

[95] Jim Crow in the 21st century: Biden denounces Georgia Republicans over new voting law, Levine, Sam, the guardian.org, March 26, 2021.

President Biden would say, that's malarkey. Everyone in America needs an ID to do almost everything – board an airplane, open a bank account, get a COVID-19 vaccine, drive a car, cash a check, buy alcohol, buy a firearm, etc. All the African Americans I have encountered are as capable of obtaining an ID as any other American. Stop insulting them.

My second thought is about Jim Crow. I will spend a little time on the subject for those who might not know about the Jim Crow laws. The Jim Crow laws were in force in the South and some border states from 1877 through the mid-1960s. They were in place to maintain racial segregation after the Civil War ended.[96] Below are examples of Jim Crow Laws:[97]

- Freedmen were not to be taught to read or write.
- Public facilities were segregated.
- Violators of these laws were subject to being whipped or branded.
- No negro who is not in the military service shall be allowed to carry firearms, or weapons of any kind.
- Marriage between whites and Negroes or Indians or persons of Negro or Indian descent to third generation are prohibited.
- White and black children shall be taught in separate schools.

The following are ways people were kept from voting:[98]

- Violence – Blacks who tried to vote were threatened, beaten, or killed.
- Literacy tests – many people were illiterate.
- Property tests – only property owners could vote.
- Grandfather clause – People who could not read and owned property were allowed to vote if their fathers or grandfathers had voted before 1867.

---

[96] A Brief history or Jim Crow Laws, USC Online Master of Laws (LLM) and Certificate Programs.
[97] Black Code and Jim Crow Law examples – Black Codes and Jim Crow (google.com).
[98] https://www.abnmuseum.org, Voting Rights For Blacks and Poor Whites in The Jim Crow South, Scholar-Griot: Russell Brooker, PhD.

- Purges – From time to time, white officials purged the voting rolls and if they arrived at the polls and found they were not registered, they could not register again until after the election.
- Poll taxes – people had to pay a tax to vote. The taxes were $25-$50 in today's dollars. Many were too poor to pay the tax.

There are also the stories of blacks being required to count soap bubbles or state the number of jellybeans in a jar. I could not find a reference to authenticate those actions, but I do not doubt that they occurred.

Now I must ask, does requiring an ID to vote in modern America sound anything like the Jim Crow Laws listed above? NO! Not even close. The comments about Jim Crow are nothing but lies and propaganda.

I could not find a reference for this statement, but I believe it whole heartedly: Propaganda and censorship are not the tools of a winning, inspirational movement. They're the weapons of bullies and tyrants.

ACTIONS

1. Don't believe everything you see, hear or read.
2. Recognize that most businesses and politicians use propaganda.
3. Propaganda is a mild form of telling blatant lies.
4. Fact-check statements.
5. Think for yourself.
6. Critical thinking is necessary to separate fact from fiction.
7. If someone tells you to only read what they tell you to read – read it. Then, more importantly, read what they tell you not to read along with what you want to read.

CHAPTER NINE

Systemic Racism/ White Supremacy

When I listen to, watch, or read the news today I am led to believe that the root of all evil in America is white supremacy and the systemic racism it created. I deferred writing about systemic racism and white supremacy until now because the decimation of the Constitution, partisan politics, government overreach, wokeism, cancel culture, and propaganda have had limited news coverage, and they deserved top billing.

Encyclopedia Britannica describes white supremacy as, "Beliefs and ideas purporting natural superiority of the lighter-skinned, or 'white,' human races over other racial groups. In contemporary usage, the term *white supremacist* has been used to describe some groups of ultranationalists, racist, or fascist doctrines. White supremacist groups often have relied on violence to achieve their goals."[99] This belief was generally taken for granted by political leaders in America and Europe through the mid-20th century. They had an obligation to civilize non-whites through imperialism. There were even scientists that tried to show there were differences in the intelligence of whites and Africans.

In America, following the Civil War, we had the Jim Crow years of legalized racial segregation and the rise of violent groups like the Ku Klux Klan (KKK). These beliefs fell into disfavor in the late 1950s and early

---

[99] White supremacy, Encyclopaedia Britannica, https://britannica.com/topic/white-supremacy, April 19, 2021.

1960s and civil rights legislation was passed – the Civil Rights Act (1964) and the Voting Rights Act (1964). Since then, we have experienced "white power" and "black power" groups, re-emergence of the KKK, neo-Nazi groups, and a Christian identity movement.

Michael Brendan Dougherty of National Review writes, "Freudianism, economics, Marxist theories of history's inevitable turns, all have become the single-cause explanation of every wicked deed or act. But lately another obsession is taking over our intellectual class. It explains every inequity in our society, and every unjust act. It's white supremacy."[100]

Jennifer Ho, a professor at the University of Colorado, explains, "that even anti-Asian hatred is rooted in white supremacy, and that white supremacy is to blame for attacks on Asians, even attacks by non-whites."[101] COVID-19 has heightened anti-Asian bigotries, "but it is not a 'white supremacist idea' to blame China for the coronavirus. It is also a Chinese idea. Taiwan still calls COVID-19 the 'Wuhan pneumonia.'"[102]

Sociologist Joe Feagin explains, "Systemic racism includes the complex array of antiblack practices, the unjustly gained political-economic power of whites, the continuing economic and other resource inequalities along racial lines, and the white racist ideologies and attitudes created to maintain and rationalize white privilege and power. Systemic here means that the core racist realities are manifested in each of society's...each major part of U.S. society – the economy, politics, education, religion, the family"[103]

Not everyone believes America is systemically racist. According to Robert W. Merry, "A lot of Americans see it as a racial assault and a huge power grab. The cry of 'systemic racism' constitutes a threat to white people. We all know that racism is the country's most potent social taboo. Even innocent slips of the tongue or benign observations can bring severe opprobrium, societal and professional sanctions, ostracism."[104] Merry continues, "But, if America is infected with systemic racism, who

---

[100] Seeing White Supremacy Everywhere, Dougherty, Michael Brendan, National Review Online, April 14, 2021.

[101] Ibid.

[102] Ibid.

[103] Definition of Systemic Racism in Sociology, Beyond Prejudice and Micro-Aggressions, Cole, Nicki Lisa, PhD, July 21, 2020.

[104] What Is 'Systemic Racism,' Really?, Merry, Robert W., theamericanconservative.com, June 8, 2020.

are the systemic racists? Certainly not, in the view of those pushing the liberal narrative, themselves. Not the cable news liberals who toss out the allegation with abandon. Not the mandarins of Hollywood who spout out about it constantly. Not the think tank mavens with their phony studies and charts. Not the Democrat establishment persistently leveraging identity politics. Not the professional celebs whose household recognition qualify them, in their view, as authority figures. Not those in the top level of the meritocratic elite living their pristine lives in gated communities. And certainly not the nation's minorities, spoon-fed the liberal narrative every day."[105]

A final quote from Merry sums it up, "Who's left? Middle-class and working-class whites, already beleaguered economically by the hollowing out of the nation's industrial base and struggling to survive in the new service and high-tech environment. And now they have to worry about becoming the next Exhibit A in the elite's persistent search for evidence of systemic racism. Deplorables again."[106]

I will spare you the agony of having to reading an exhaustive list of the landmark African American legislation affecting African American lives, Constitutional Clauses, Ratified Amendments, Federal Court Decisions, and Executive Orders and Proclamations. If you are interested, you can hop on the internet and access the lists from Wikipedia, the free encyclopedia.

I am tired of this mountain of hog wash. Systemic Racism was refuted long ago. A nation ruled by systemic racism would not have elected and re-elected a black man president. It took millions of "white" voters to do it. If systemic racism runs rampant, why do we have so many minority police officers, elected officials, minority doctors and lawyers, business owners, and super-star athletes? Enough of the BS!

The cry of systemic racism is destroying our country. It is turning us into hate groups. We are being driven into tribes of color, race, ethnicity, religion, liberals, and conservatives that hate each other. Combine white supremacy with wokeism, cancel culture and a partisan power grab and you have the formula for the demise of the American dream.

In addition to that, China, Russia, North Korea, Iran, and our allies are watching very closely. Sumantra Maitra writes, "It's a cliché to claim

---

[105] Ibid.
[106] Ibid.

every setback as the official end of unipolarity, but if there were ever to be a date for historians to mark the televised humiliation and official end of American hegemon, it would be the very public verbal slapping of U.S. Secretary of State Antony Blinken and National Secretary Advisor Jake Sullivan by the Chinese ambassador on U.S. soil."[107] The March 19, 2021, meeting in Anchorage, Alaska included a speech by China's top diplomat, Jang Jiechi, about the United States' struggling democracy, poor treatment of minorities, and criticizing its foreign and trade policies. He accused the United States of failing in racial justice and that our representatives were not speaking from a position of strength.

On June 16, 1858, Abraham Lincoln accepted the Illinois Republican Party's nomination as the state's U.S. Senator. His acceptance speech included, "A house divided against itself, cannot stand." It was true before the Civil War, and it is equally true today. We either come together, or our America will fall.

ACTIONS

1. There are words, such as the diminutive "ni**er" and actions, such as excluding non-whites, that demonstrate you are 'racist' to minorities – be aware of what you say and do.
2. When you hear a public figure blaming white supremacy and/or racism for something, use letters, phone calls, and social media to "call them out."
3. Use letters, phone calls, and social media to contact businesses claiming racism is the "cause" of some unfortunate incident.
4. Do not vote for politicians who blame "racism" when it cannot be proven to be true.
5. Remember, saying something is racist, does not make it true.
6. Contact media outlets that use racism as the reason for our problems.
7. Stop subscriptions to magazines that blame our country's woes on racism.

---

[107] It's No Surprise China Employs The Anti-American Propaganda of Systemic Racism, Maitra Sumantra, The Federalist, March 22, 2012.

CHAPTER TEN

LGBTQ

I had an uncle who loved me! It is not unusual for an uncle to love a nephew, but I did not understand how he loved me until I was 23 years old.

When I was five or six years old, I started collecting figurines of dogs. I was seven when my parents and I were visiting my aunt and uncle in their antique shop. I saw a set of dog figurines that I just had to have for my collection. It was a mother with several of her pups. My mother asked my uncle how much they cost, and he said, two. I remember saying to my mother, "We can afford that." She then explained that they were not two dollars; they were 200 dollars.

Before we left the shop, my uncle took me over to the shelf where the dogs were and put them in my shirt pocket. When we got home and my mother saw them, she immediately called my uncle and told him I had stolen the dogs and she would bring them right back to him. He told her not to bring them back, that he had given them to me, and he wanted me to have them for my collection.

As I grew, my uncle hired me to do various things like yard work and setting nails in a new floor he had installed. When I was 16 or 17, he had me drive him on a three- or four-day antique buying trip. When I was 23, he paid me $100 a month to tutor him in algebra. A few months into the tutoring is when he kissed me on the lips and touched me inappropriately.

It was not until then that I realized he was gay and that he may have been in love with me since he gave me those dogs 16 years earlier. I was extremely naive. All the signs had been there for several years, but I never paid any attention to that "stuff." My attitude was, and still is, I do not care if someone is gay, just do not push it on me. My uncle attempted to push his sexuality on me, I rejected it, and that algebra tutoring session was the last time I saw him.

Although I severed the relationship, I had great empathy for my uncle. I think about the many years he worked up to that moment and how heartbreaking my rejection must have been. I still think about it often even though he died more than 20 years ago. I empathize with those LGBTQ persons and the struggles they must be experiencing.

LGBTQ issues are confusing and hard to understand, especially for the older generations. The Bible defines marriage in Genesis 2:24 as a union between one man and one woman. This is upheld in Matthew 19:5 and Ephesians 5:31. Any sexual activity that takes place outside of this context is treated as sinful. Jesus calls it "sexual immorality" in Mark 7:21. Romans 1:24-32 treats both male and female same-sex practices as sinful. This makes it extremely hard for many that live a strict moral life to accept LGBTQ practices.

Regardless of how strongly some people might feel about specific passages in the Bible, they must also understand that GOD DON'T MAKE JUNK! So, with the understanding that it is okay to be straight, lesbian, gay, bisexual, transgender, queer, or questioning, I will dig into the various issues.

Biologically there are two sexes – male and female. Females have XX chromosomes and men have XY chromosomes. Except in rare conditions like hermaphroditism, males have testes and produce testosterone and females have ovaries and produce estrogen. Hence, when you are born, sexually, you are a boy or a girl.

Gender makes things a little more complicated. Gender refers "to the cultural differences expected (by society/culture) of men and women according to their sex. A person's sex does not change from birth, but their gender can."[108] Dr. Saul McLeod explains that "the evolutionary approach argues that gender role division appears as an adaptation to the challenges faced by ancestral humans in the EEA (the environment of evolutionary adaption).[109] Men were hunters and women took care of the home and

---

[108] Biological Theories of Gender, Mcleod, Dr. Saul, Simply Psychology, 2014.
[109] Ibid.

looked after the children. This also protected the reproduction cycle by protecting women from the dangers of hunting and gathering food. The hormones influence brain and body development, but I do not want to get into too much biology at this point - a little later.

I assume most people can define the elements of the LBGTQ acronym, but for those who cannot, I will keep it simple and brief. Lesbian – women are attracted to women. Gay – men are attracted to men. Bisexual – a person who is attracted to both sexes. Transgender – a person whose gender identity is different from that generally associated with his/her biological sex. Queer – an older term used to refer to a person whose sexual orientation is not exclusively heterosexual. Questioning – a person who cannot decide their sexual orientation or gender identity.

Here is one more attempt to differentiate between gender identity and sexual orientation. Bali White says gender identity refers, "to a person's internal sense of their role in their culture's system defining the traditional behavioral differences between men and women."[110] White continues with a definition of sexual orientation, "which is the emotional and sexual attraction they feel for others."[111]

Kenya Evelyn reports that new a new Gallup survey shows that "5.6% of American adults, an estimated 18 million, identify as LGBTQ."[112] Evelyn reports that "54.6% of respondents identified as bisexual, 24.5% as gay, 11.7% as lesbian, and 11.3% as transgender."[113]

There are certainly social issues affecting the adult LGBTQ community, but my focus is on our young people. The *Journal of Adolescent Health*, study of LGBTQ+ suicide statistics found "that adolescents aged 12 to 14 who identify as lesbian, gay, bisexual, and/or transgender are more likely to die by suicide than heterosexual teens of the same age.[114] A 2018 study found that LGBTQ+ teenagers are three times as likely to attempt suicide as their heterosexual peers. The study reports that "a full 40% of homeless

---

[110] Lesbian, Gay, Bisexual, Transgender – What's the difference?, White, Bali, The Guardian, April 18, 2017.

[111] Ibid.

[112] New record as estimated 18m Americans identify as LGBTQ, poll finds, Evelyn, Kenya, in *Washington*, February 24, 2021.

[113] Ibid.

[114] LGBTQ+ Suicide Statistics Show Greater Risk Among Young Teens, Newport Academy, May 6, 2019.

youth are LGBTQ+ teens who have been kicked out of the house."[115] Other significant findings about LGBTQ+ youth in schools include: threats with weapons on school property, bullying in school, and cyberbullying.

These reports beg the question, where does LGBTQ education belong? It appears to me that if 40% of the homeless youth are LGBTQ teens who have been kicked out of the house, there are a lot of parents who cannot find it in their hearts to support their children through that difficult period in their lives. Can churches help? Some can, but with church participation sharply declining, they cannot make much of a dent in the problem. That leaves us with the schools, and that, to me, is problematic.

First, most of the children in school are not LGBTQ. Should all children be subject to sexual identity and gender identity classes? If so, at what age and to what degree and intensity? Second, I hate to say it, but I do not trust the schools to teach social issues without bias. Educators for Social Change lists lesson plan resources including: Teaching Tolerance Gender Lesson Plans (30 lesson plans about gender), Lesson Plans to Help Students Understand Gender and to Support Transgender and Non-Binary Children, and I Am Who I Am, that teaches sixth and seventh graders how to differentiate between gender identity, gender expression, and sexual orientation.

Schools should focus on teaching children how to think, not what to think. School curricula should not focus on affecting social change. There is not an easy answer, but everyone needs to be thinking and having rational conversations about how to tackle the problem.

I said it before, but I will say it again – what gays, lesbians, and bisexuals do is their business, just do not push it on me. But it is not the gay, lesbian, and bisexual issues driving the social agenda – it is the transgender issue. It is an issue that involves a small percent of the population, but it is tearing the country apart.

Soon after he was inaugurated, President Biden signed an executive order mandating that federal agencies take actions to make sure "children" are allowed to play on the sports team and use the locker room and restroom that accords with their gender identity. That means boys who identify as girls can use the girls' restroom. I was shocked to learn that a 2019 Harvard CAPS/Harris Poll found 54% supported such a law. That

---

[115] Ibid.

frightened me, but what shocked the hell out of me was that 44% said the Supreme Court should rule on the matter. It is hard for me to believe that Americans want the Supreme Court to decide how we should function as a society. We are allowing an exceedingly small group of people to define what our culture and mores should be. Is that the America we want?

Justice Neil Gorsuch has said the word "sex" in Title VII of the 1964 Civil Rights Act should be understood to include "sexual orientation" and "gender identity." Gorsuch was appointed by President Trump and is supposedly a Constitutionalist. "Sexual orientation" was barely discussed in the 1960s and "gender identity" was only popularized by the feminist movement in the 1970s. If the Congress wanted those issues in the Act, they would have included them.

The "Definitions" section of Title VII includes the following: "The terms 'because of sex' or 'on the basis of sex' include, but are not limited to, because of pregnancy, childbirth, or related medical conditions; and women affected by pregnancy, childbirth, or related medical conditions shall be treated the same for all employment-related purposes..." I remember the debates surrounding Title VII and they were about the equality of opportunity in the workplace for minorities and women. References to women were clearly about XX chromosome women because of the language about pregnancy, childbirth, etc. Justice Gorsuch's opinion is an excellent example of legislating from the bench – acting more like lawmakers than judges whose job is to interpret the law as written, not to determine the intent of the lawmakers. This issue belongs in the Congress! Congress can amend Title VII. People want to leave it to the Supreme Court because they do not have the guts to hold rational discussions and make the elected officials cast votes. The Equality Act would make gender identity a protected class under the Civil Rights Act of 1964. At this point the language does not clearly define what gender identity is. Will our legislators grow spines, debate the issue and do what they need to do? It does not look like it as they have not shown spines on many other critical issues.

Studies are evolving about whether transgender athletes, especially transgender women and girls, have an advantage when taking part in women's sporting events. The NCAA has weighed in by demanding that events be withdrawn from states that have passes or are considering laws that ban transgender women and girls from participating in sports. I do not have a problem with leaving transgender policies at the college and professional levels to their respective organizations. I do have a problem with removing those policies at the K-12 level out of the hands of the local communities, schools, and states.

My opposition to the transgender and the use of restrooms and locker rooms is about safety. This is especially important at the grammar and high school levels. My opposition does not have anything to do animosity toward those who identify as transgender. I am worried about the advantage it may give to potential predators. There is not a clear definition or understanding about what "gender identity" is. Is it enough to just say, "I am a girl or woman?" If so, someone could be a boy or man one day, a girl or woman the next, and a boy or man again the following day. It is a very loosey-goosey concept to me.

C. Douglas Golden reports that, "In Decatur, Georgia, the school district settled a case with the Department of Education in June after the department found the school district didn't appropriately investigate a sexual assault allegation made in 2017 in which a 5-year-old girl was allegedly sexually assaulted by a boy using the girls bathroom."[116] Golden continues, "The Office of Civil Rights...came to conflicting conclusions on whether the boy identified as transgender or 'gender fluid'."[117] Because of the school's policy on transgender students, students are allowed to select the bathrooms of their choice. That policy has been rescinded but here comes the Equity Act.

I agree with Golden when he says, "Schools, shelters, gyms and other organizations need the ability to set rules to protect those they serve. This fact ought to be independent of how politicians feel regarding transgender issues."[118]

I can summarize my position very simply – KEEP BOYS OUT OF MY GRANDDAUGHTERS' BATHROOMS AND LOCKER ROOMS! If you agree, you better start speaking up!

---

[116] God Help Us: Biden to Allow Males in Girls Bathrooms on Day One, Golden, C. Douglas, The Western Journal, January 20, 2021.

[117] Ibid.

[118] Ibid.

ACTIONS

1. Give studied thought to the LGBTQ issues.
2. Prepare yourself to discuss issues with facts, not just emotions.
3. Learn about how your schools are addressing "sexual identity" and "gendered identity."
4. You elect school board members – vote only for those who support your position on LGBTQ issues.
5. Write, call, and email your state and federal elected officials and let them know loud and clear how you feel about Equity Act and other LGBTQ issues.
6. Be sure your schools are taking serious actions to stop bullying of all types.
7. Do not disparage those who identify as LGBTQ.

CHAPTER ELEVEN

Law and Order, BLM, and Defund Police

I was angry on June 16, 2020, when I wrote Part One of what became a four-part dissertation entitled, "This is Not a Time for Cowardice." I wrote Parts Two, Three, and Four over the following few days. I never did anything with them, never showed them to anyone, and had forgotten about them until they turned up in a stack of papers I was going through preparing for this chapter. Hopping on the computer and writing "stuff" is how I frequently ventilate my feelings. It may not accomplish much but it is sure better than participating in violent protests.

The following is what I wrote as Part One. Note that my comments are not supported by formal references but if pressed, I am sure I could find them:

"It is dangerous to speak out about mob violence, but if we don't, we may well lose the Great American Experiment. Since I am retired, I do not have to worry about being disciplined or fired by my employer, but I may make enemies s and lose friends – so be it!

I believe it is universally agreed that black lives do matter, and the horrific death of George Floyd (a convicted felon) demands that we change. But my question is which black lives matter? David Dorn was an African American, 77-year-old retired police captain who was killed (reportedly by a young black man) while protecting a store during the George Floyd protests in St. Louis. There were five hours of TV coverage of Floyd's funeral, but I could only find one minute of coverage of Dorn's. Didn't Dorn's life matter as much as Floyd's?

Black store owners lost everything during the "mostly peaceful" George Floyd protests the summer of 2020. I do not see mainstream media covering those lives. Don't their lives matter? How about the people who bought their groceries or had prescriptions filled at those stores - don't their lives matter?

On May 31, 2020 in Chicago, police were overwhelmed handling protest rioting and looting all over the city. There were no police in the poorest neighborhoods. There were 65,000 calls to 911 which was 50,000 higher than normal, and it was the deadliest day in 60 years with 18 murders – 8 more than the number of unarmed African Americans killed by police in all of 2020. Do the lives of ordinary citizens matter?

In Washington, D.C. only 23% of black children are proficient in reading. Do those lives matter?

African Americans are twice as likely to take out predatory payday loans that keep them in financial crisis. Do those lives matter?

In New York City more African American babies are aborted each year than are born alive. Do those lives matter?"[119]

I will say it here and will say it again, black lives matter and so do all lives. The fact that black lives matter is indisputable. The Black Lives Matter movement (BLM), however, is corrupt and destructive. The social movement was formed in 2013 to fight racism and the unjust killing of Black people by police. BLM was cofounded by three Black community organizers – Patrisse Khan-Cullors, Alicia Garza and Opal Tometi. [120]

BLM was a response to George Zimmerman, a neighborhood watch volunteer, who was acquitted on charges stemming from his fatal shooting of Trayvon Martin, in February 2012. BLM protested the deaths of several Black people by police including Eric Garner, Michael Brown, Sandra Bland, Philando Castile, Freddie Gray, Laquan McDonald, Tamir Rice, Walter Scott, Alton Sterling, and Breonna Taylor. Each of these "victims" is a story with many relevant facts that influenced the police action that

---

[119] This is Not a Time for Cowardice – Part one, personal thoughts written by John D. Sanderson, June 16, 2020.
[120] https://www.britannica.com/topic/Black-Lives-Matter, August, 13, 2020.

took their lives. They should not be lumped together and erroneously reported as proof that police are hunting black people.

After a March 29, 2021, foot chase, 13-year-old Adam Toledo was shot and killed by a Chicago police officer. The police were responding to a report of shots being fired about 2:30 in the morning and a chase ensued. Video shows the youth had a gun in his hand while being chased and when he stopped by a fence, the gun was still in his hand. As Toledo turned toward the officer, he flipped the gun behind the fence and showed his hands. The officer had 0.8 seconds to make a shoot or do not shoot decision.

Other than while studying the entire video, the only picture I have seen on the mainstream media is that of Toledo standing with his hands in the air. The reporters call the shooting an "unjustified" shooting of a black man. I have not heard any of them question why a 13-year-old was out at 2:30 in the morning with a 21-year-old gang member. If he had been home in bed where he should have been, he would still be alive. Where were his parents or other responsible adults in his life?

A 20-year-old African American man, Daunte Wright, was fatally shot during a traffic stop. Wright was driving with an expired license plate and the police discovered that a "gross misdemeanor warrant" had been issued for his arrest. Wright resisted the arrest and was accidently shot by a police officer who thought she was holding a taser, not a gun. A terrible mistake but not one that did not warrant the headline, "Daunte Wright was stopped for expired plates, but driving while Black may have been his 'crime'."[121] Statements like that fan the flames of discontent while doing nothing to address the real problems of policing. If Daunte Wright had not resisted arrest, he would be alive today.

Thirty minutes before the April 20, 2021, verdict on the Derek Chauvin murder of George Floyd was announced, Ma'Khia Bryant was shot by a police officer in Columbus, Ohio. The officer was responding to a 911 call and video shows Bryant holding a large knife and preparing to lunge the knife into a woman pinned against an automobile. Again, we hear cries of another senseless killing of a black woman at the hands of a white police officer. There will be a formal investigation, but I have

---

[121] Daunte Wright was stopped for expired plates, but driving while Black may have been his 'crime,' Siemasko, Corky, NBC News, April 13, 2021.

viewed the video several times and the officer had a split second to decide, "Do I shoot the girl with the knife or let her kill the other girl?" He shot one black girl to save another black girl. Professional basketball player LeBron James responded to the shooting by posting a picture of the police officer that shot Ma'Khia and added the words "YOU'RE NEXT #ACCOUNTABILITY." Such a posting is divisive and endangers the life of a police officer. The actions of professional athletes like James and Kaepernick, along with major league baseball moving the all-star game out of Georgia, are why I, and many others, switch channels when their games come on TV.

Whitehouse Press Secretary Jen Psaki said, "Our focus is on working to address systemic racism and implicit bias head on and, of course to passing laws and legislation that will put much-needed reforms into place at police departments around the country."[122] The shooting was certainly tragic, but the police officer was in a no-win situation – one of the girls was going to die. On her television show, *The View*, Joy Behar, said the police officer should have shot into the air, or shot Bryant in the leg or butt to stop the fight. Shooting a firearm in the air is dangerous if not illegal - the bullet must come down somewhere and police are trained to shoot at body mass - not legs or butts. I did not hear Behar ask about the foster care Bryant had been in or about her mother or aunt both of whom were interviewed about the incident. The police cannot be held at fault for everything. The foster care program and the community also has some culpability.

In an article reviewed by Allen Collins in Smithsonian NMNH, states jellyfish have survived 500 million years. Jellyfish have survived this long without a brain – I pray that Behar and her "blame the police for everything" ilk do not fare as well.

BLM protests took on a new dimension with the May 25, 2020, death of George Floyd. The last 9 minutes and 30 seconds of Floyd's death was videoed by a bystander and was repeatedly aired on television nationwide. What happened to Mr. Floyd was horrendous and the country was united in believing it should not have happened. Derek Chauvin, the police officer who held his knee on Floyd's neck, even pleaded guilty to a charge of Murder 3. He knew he was wrong.

---

[122] 10TV Web Staff, Associated Press, 3:37 PM EDT, April 21, 2021.

Floyd's death created protests all over the country and the cries of "systemic racism," "defund the police," and "White supremacy" were shouted daily, not just at the protests, but in the newspapers and on television. There have been "hate each other" and "hate America" movements for decades but they have taken on lives that I could never have imagined. BLM fund raising gained momentum and the Black Lives Matter Global Network Foundation (BLMGNF) reported that it raised over $90 million in 2020.

Do not get me wrong. There is nothing wrong with fund raising – I did it myself for a hospital, childcare center, art museum, community college, and a university. My concern is about what the money is used for. Mike Gonzalez reports that in a 2015 interview of BLM leaders Alicia Garza, Patrisse Cullors and Opal Tometiln, Cullors said, "Myself and Alicia in particular are trained organizers. We are trained Marxists."[123] Are donations going to fund Marxist organizations that want to completely transform America? Gonzalez further reports that if you read a list of demands on the BLM website you will see:

- "We disrupt the Western-prescribed nuclear-family-structure requirement by supporting each other as extended families and 'villages' that collectively care for one another."[124]
- BLM partner organization, M4BL, calls for abolishing all police and prisons along with a 'progressive restructuring of tax codes at the local, state and federal levels to ensure a radical and sustainable redistribution of wealth."[125]
- Another M4BL demand is "the retroactive decriminalization, immediate release and record expungement of all drug-related offences and prostitution and reparations for the devastating impact of the 'war on drugs' and criminalization of prostitution."[126]

---

[123] The Agenda of Black Lives Matter Is Far Different From the Slogan, Gonzalea, Mike, The Heritage Foundation, July 3, 2020.
[124] Ibid.
[125] Ibid.
[126] Ibid.

On another note, BLM co-founder Patrisse Khan-Cullors recently purchased a $1.4 million home in an exclusive, majority white Los Angeles neighborhood. She has spent $3.2 million acquiring homes in the last few years. Apparently transforming America pays well.

While BLM was raising money to radically transform America, cities were in chaos and businesses were destroyed. Protesters in Seattle, Washington, took over part of the city and dubbed it and "Autonomous Zone" that is free of police. Major damage was done during protests to government buildings, stores, and neighborhoods in Portland, Seattle, Chicago, Minneapolis, and other cities. Mainstream media called them "mostly peaceful" protests that caused up to $2 Billion in damage.[127] That report was from September 2020, and we may never know what the final total will be. And that is only the financial damage - there is no way to quantify the damage to the lives of those who lived, worked, or owned businesses in the riot areas. There has been a 10% increase in murders in cities that saw BLM protests. When buildings and businesses are destroyed by protesters, they are not peaceful. If police are given stand down orders and allow protesters to destroy property, we do not have law and order.

In the George Floyd case, Derek Chauvin was charged with three counts: Second-degree unintentional murder, third-degree murder, and second-degree manslaughter. His trial ended with a guilty verdict on three counts. Most people agreed that he was guilty although some may argue he was overcharged.

I believe Chauvin was guilty, but what I am not sure of is whether he had a fair trial. Gary Schrader says justice is "the administration of law; the quality of being just, impartial, or fair; the quality of conforming to law."[128]

In his letter from Birmingham Jail, Dr. Martin Luther King wrote "Injustice anywhere is a threat to justice everywhere. We are caught in an inescapable network of mutuality, tied in a single garment of destiny. Whatever affects one directly, affects all indirectly."[129]

Chauvin's trial was held in Minneapolis, the city where the alleged (alleged before the trial) crime was committed. The video of the event was

---

[127] George Floyd Riots Caused Record-Setting $2 Billion in Damage, New Report Says, Polumbo, Brad, Foundation for Economic Education, September 16, 2020.
[128] Schrader, Gary, Equal Justice, April 18, 2021.
[129] Ibid.

shown on television news programs hundreds, if not thousands, of times making it almost impossible to find jurors who were not fully aware of the incident. To add insult to injury, the City of Minneapolis announced a $27 million settlement with Floyd's family during the jury selection process. Once selected, the jurors were not sequestered and could see and were exposed to all the news coverage and the comments being made about it. Stores were boarded up and the police and national guard were in place in the event a "guilty of murder" verdict was not reached.

While the trial was in progress, Representative Maxine Waters, D-California, asked for police protection during her trip to Minnesota where she said to BLM protesters, "I hope we get a verdict that says guilty, guilty, guilty and, if we don't...we've got to stay on the street. We have to get more active; we have to get more confrontational."[130] Her attempt at jury intimidation infuriated Hennepin County District Judge Peter Cahill who was presiding over the trial said, "I wish elected officials would stop talking about this case especially in a manner that is disrespectful to the rule of law. I'll give you that Congresswoman Water may have given you something on an appeal that may result in this whole trial being overturned."[131]

Representative Waters has a history of calling for aggressive action and harassment. In 2018, she encouraged people to harass members of the Trump administration. "If you see anybody from that cabinet in a restaurant, in a department store, at a gas station, you get out and create a crowd. And you tell them they're not welcome anymore."[132]

President Biden even weighed in while the Chauvin jury was deliberating. He said, "I'm praying the verdict is the right verdict, which is—I think it's overwhelming, in my view." The President did not say what he thought the right verdict was, but it is obvious to the most casual of observers that he was advocating for a guilty verdict. Of all people, the

---

[130] Hypocrite Maxine Waters Sought Police Escort to Cop-Bashing BLM Rally, https://headlineusa.com/maxine-police-escort-blm-rally/?utm_source=HUSAemail&utm_medium=email&utm_campaign=HUSAemail, April 20, 2021.

[131] Chauvin Trial Judge: Maxine Waters' Statement 'May Overturn This Whole Trial', Dawson, Greg, True Conservative Hub, April 20, 2021.

[132] Maxine Waters's Long History of Reckless Rhetoric, Perkins, Joseph, Wall Street Journal, April 23, 2021.

President should be advocating for a fair trial and for equal justice under the law, not drawing conclusions before a verdict is in.

Speaker of the House, Nancy Pelosi, made one of the most egregious comments I heard from any of the politicians. During a press conference held by the Congressional Black Caucus outside the U.S. Capitol building in Washington, D.C., Pelosi looked heavenward and said, "Thank you, George Floyd, for sacrificing your life for justice...your name will always be synonymous with justice." I do not know if she was recommending him for sainthood or martyrdom. A martyr is a person who is killed because of their religious or other beliefs. Floyd was tragically killed because he passed a phony $20 and resisted arrest. A saint must have three miracles attributed to him/her. George Floyd was not a saint – he was convicted of eight crimes, mostly for drug and theft charges, and served four years in jail after accepting a plea bargain for a 2007 aggravated robbery in a home invasion. Geroge Floyd did not deserve to die the way he did but let us not make him into hero, saint, or martyr.

It was recently revealed that an alternate juror in the George Floyd case said, "I did not want to go through rioting and destruction again and I was concerned about people coming to my house if they were not happy with the verdict."[133] The alternate juror had no say in the case, but her comment demonstrates the impact of widespread news coverage showing jury intimidation. Everyone deserves a fair trial and jurors must be allowed to make decisions based on the facts presented to them without fear of reprisal.

According to an article in American News, BLM's response to the Chauvin trial verdict is not encouraging. In Minneapolis, the city where George Floyd was killed, a member of BLM proclaimed, "They gonna let us burn this whole motherf**ker to the ground before they give us some systemic change."[134] Another protester said," We're not gonna stop just because we got one conviction. We are never going to be satisfied."[135] A BLM protester in New York told white people dining outside to, "stay

---

[133] Yuccas, Jamie, Novak Analisa, CBS News, April 23, 2021, 6:41 AM.
[134] 'We are never going to be satisfied': BLM Minneapolis responds to Chauvin verdict, American News, April 20, 2021.
[135] Ibid.

the f**k out of New York! We don't want your money; we don't want you here, we don't want your f**kin' taquerias owned by f**kin' white men."[136]

It is time that we focus on the March 5, 1987, words of Ronald Reagan when he said, "We must reject the idea that every time a law's broken, society is guilty rather than the lawbreaker. It is time to restore the American precept that each individual is accountable for his actions."

There are police officers that should not be carrying guns or wearing the police uniform. The 'bad apples' need to be searched out and removed from police forces. Police misconduct needs to be identified and punished. Use of force policies need to be reviewed and updated as new information and technology becomes available, but this needs to be done at the local level, not by federal agencies. As our federal agencies get more involved in how local police operate, we move closer to the federalizing of the police. Federalizing police is what happened in Nazi Germany and is in place today in countries like China, North Korea, and Russia. Federalizing the police places Orwell's <u>1984</u> just around the corner.

Another horrendous thing is happening. Year to date, homicides are up 33% in Chicago, 36% in New York City, 33% in Philadelphia and 31% in Washington, D.C. Is that the country you want to live in? New York Police Departments retirements and announced departures were 5,300+ in 2020, up 75% from 2019. This is occurring throughout the country.

Regardless of the reforms that may take place, there is only one sure-fire, 100% guaranteed to work, infallible way to prevent another George Floyd type incident – the police stop apprehending lawbreakers. But is this what we want? BLM does not represent most of the Black citizenry. BLM calls for defunding of the police while, according to an August 5, 2020, Newsweek report, 81% of the Black Americans do not want less police presence despite protests, some want more. Many Blacks, however, are being misled by rhetoric designed to create discord.

Greg Piper reports that a survey shows Blacks wildly overestimate the frequency police fatally shoot young black men. Piper continues, "Eight in 10 black survey respondents said they believe young black men are more likely to die in police shootings than in traffic accidents."[137] Traffic accidents kill about 23 in 100,000 men ages 25-29, with a slightly higher

---

[136] Ibid.
[137] Piper, Greg, Just the News, April 19, 2021.

rate for blacks over whites. This is at least five times higher than police killings of black men of the same age, using any method of force.[138]

The Washington Post reports that in 2020 there were a total of 1,021 fatal police shootings, 243 of which were black. The Chicago Sun-Times reports that in 2020 there were 576 black people were murdered not by police. Tom Trinko estimates that" in the last three years in Chicago, there have been 11.8 murders for every American soldier killed in Afghanistan."[139]

On April 24, 2021, Jesse Watters, host of 'Watters' World' reported that "Last year, there were 50 million interactions between police and suspects, and 10 million arrests. Out of that, 18 unarmed black Americans were fatally shot by police, and 24 unarmed White Americans. An unarmed Black American who a police officer makes contact with has a 0.000036% chance of being fatally shot." This is not to say that racism does not exist or that police do not fatally shoot too many people. It does mean that the police are not hunting down blacks to shoot as BLM and other defund police groups have claimed. I do not have the statistics to back it up, but I am willing to bet most of those shootings would be averted if people did not attack police or resist arrest.

On August 3, 2020, NBC Channel 5 out of Chicago reported 38 juveniles were killed by gun violence in Chicago so far this year and five were under the age of 10. Everyone knows the name George Floyd, but how many know the names of 9-year-old Janari Ricks or 7-year-old Natalie Wallace, or 10-year-old Lina Nunez, or 1-year-old Sincere Gaston, or 3-year-old Mekhi James? There is a database available at www.chicagotribune.com that lists the names of shooting victims back to 2016. The media does not give these deaths the time of day, so my belief is that only the family and close friends know those names. These names and hundreds of others must not be forgotten because those lives matter too. If we are to have equal justice under the law, then the media and politicians must start addressing the violence occurring in our cities, especially in the minority and poor neighborhoods of our largest cities.

---

[138] Ibid.
[139] Democrats ignore mass shootings of blacks in Chicago, Trinko, Tom, American Thinker, October 30, 2019.

John D. Sanderson

Rav Arora reports that "at least 8,600 black lives were lost to homicide in 2020."[140] The national focus, however, is on the less than one half of one percent that were lost during conflicts with police. Those are the ones that fit the political narrative. Arora continues to report that in Chicago, 80% of gun-violence victims in 2020 were black and that more than 90% of black homicide victims are killed by black offenders. Neither the media nor the politicians talk about this because it does not fit their narrative that Whites are the root of all evil.

It is impossible for me to believe that we can have equal justice under the law unless we have law and order free of double standards, apolitical judges, an unbiased media and politicians that care more about America than getting re-elected to office. These obstacles may be too much to overcome, but we can at least try to minimize them.

The double standards that abound tear at the fabric of the notion that we are a country of laws. I say double standards, but it is more like quintuple standards. We have laws for Republicans, laws for Democrats, laws for the rich, laws for the Bidens, and laws for everyone else. We are a country "with" laws, but not a country of laws. To be a country of laws, the laws must be enforced, and they need to be enforced fairly and equally. There are too many high-profile politicians and celebrities that demonstrate that laws and rules are "okay for thee, but not for me." This was vividly demonstrated when California Governor Gavin Newsom attended a birthday dinner for a lobbyist. The party was held at the fancy "French Laundry" restaurant, in close quarters without social distancing or masks. This occurred when Newsom had ordered Californians to stay home due to COVID except for an essential job or to shop for essential needs.

President Biden's son, Hunter, has a history of illegal narcotic use and lied on the Firearm Transaction Record when purchasing a handgun in October 2018. Despite calls for an investigation you can take it to the bank that there will not be any investigation. However, you can also take it to the bank that if it had been Eric or Donald Trump, Jr. lying on the form, there would be an investigation. President Biden has put forth recommendations

[140] These Black Lives Didn't Seem to Matter in 2020, Arora, Rav, New York Post, February 8, 2021.

82

for enhanced background checks for gun purchases – not only a double standard but extreme hypocrisy.

Hunter Biden's "lie to try" may be a minor offense but the double standard and hypocrisy it represents is real. Other double standards are far more egregious. Take, for example, sanctuary cities and states. It is against the law to enter our country illegally, but cities and states are allowed to harbor known illegal aliens and protect them from deportation.

The riots following the death of George Floyd in 2020 demonstrate more double standards and the lack of enforcing the law. There were thousands of protests around the country and more than 90% were peaceful, but hundreds were not. Lives were lost and property losses were astronomical. Thousands of arrests were made but most were charged with low-level crimes like curfew violations.

The Department of Justice (DOJ) said during a September 25, 2020, press conference the "Violent opportunists have exploited these (George Floyd's death) demonstrations in various ways." Among those ways were attempted murder, assaulting police officers, arson, damaging federal property, and felony possession of firearms. These violent protests were mostly aligned with BLM. On September 21, 2020, the DOJ called out Democrat-run cities of New York, Portland, and Seattle for allowing anarchy to reign and refusing to undertake reasonable measures to counteract criminal activities. Kamala Harris, now our Vice President, raised money to bail protesters out of jail.

On January 6, 2021, tens of thousands of Trump supporters gathered, and Trump told them to peacefully march to the Capitol to show support for fair elections. Some right-wing extremists entered the Capitol Building in what is being called an insurrection. According to the Insider, 441 have been arrested and charged so far.

Luke Broadwater reports that The Capitol Police had clear advance warning about the potential for violence, but officers were instructed to by their leaders not to use their most aggressive tactics to hold off the mob.[141] That falls on the shoulders of whoever gave the "hold back" order, but we will never know who it was - It is too political.

---

[141] Capitol Police Told to Hold Back on Riot Response on Jan. 6, Report Finds, Broadwater, Luke, New York Times, April 13, 2021.

The FBI says that no firearms were found in the US Capitol during the January 6 incursion. If the incursion was as so many contend, an attempt to overthrow the government, why wasn't anyone entering the Capitol carrying a firearm? Does not make sense to me.

There was a shooting death in the Capitol on January 6, 2021. A U.S. Capitol Police officer shot unarmed Ashli Babbitt. He must not have understood the "hold back" order. Unlike the white officers involved with shooting black men, the Capitol Police officer has not been identified and he has been cleared in the shooting death. The shooting was video recorded by a bystander, and I have watched it many times.[142] I have included the link to that video as a footnote and encourage you watch it. When you watch it, pause at 27 seconds, and examine that frame very closely. What I see is a black hand holding the gun that shot unarmed, white, Ashli Babbitt. I could be wrong, but that is what I see. Could it be that the officer has not been identified or charged is because it does not fit the narrative? Another example of a double standard?

At the height of the BLM-Antifa riots last year, Nancy Pelosi said, "People will do what they do" when rioters ripped down a statue of Christopher Columbus and threw it in Boston Harbor. Pelosi, Biden, Harris, and others on the left, said nothing to discourage the BLM-Antifa riots last year. But when unrest came from the right, the message was that we must enforce the law and hold people accountable.

We need strong leadership to return from a country "with" laws to a country "of" laws. With the current leadership in Washington, D.C., I am saddened to say that I do not have a lot of hope, but as they say in the movie "Galaxy Quest," Never Give Up. Never Surrender.

---

[142] https://www.nbcnews.com/video/capitol-shooting-that-led-to-ashli-babbit-s-death-captured-on-video.

ACTIONS

1. Display a blue porch light to show your support for police.
2. Take snacks and electrolyte drinks to police stations – let them know you appreciate what they do.
3. Encourage your state legislators to pass an "anti-riot" bill like the one just passed in Florida. It allows local police to challenge budgets, opens cities to liability for poor riot control, and creates or strengthens penalties against rioters.
4. If you hear someone calling to defund the police, ask them who they would like to call when they are in trouble – Ghostbusters, a criminal, a meth head?
5. Make sure your local police oversight groups are doing their jobs.
6. Vote out elected officials that will not enforce laws.
7. Vote for law-and-order candidates.

CHAPTER TWELVE

Education

In 1948 we did not have kindergarten at my school. My mother was my kindergarten teacher. She taught me how to behave, tie my shoes, recite and print the ABCs, and how to count. She read books to me every day and by time I went to school I could read a few words. I had a defective "R" in my speech, and she worked with me to correct that before I entered first grade. She took me to Sunday School. My dad was great too, but he was sent overseas during WW II, so his teaching came into play when I was about six years old. More on that later. I had two older sisters and early on they taught me the ins and outs of school.

The point I am making is that family is important – mom, dad, brothers, sisters, and grandparents. Getting a child off on the right track is critical to how they develop. That is why my mother choose not to work outside the home until my sisters and I were older. We did not have a lot of "extras," but we had that which is more important than material things – we had love and caring parents that were involved in every aspect of our lives.

According to Emma Green, the family has an especially important role in a child's education. "It is a decisive importance in what will mean the social and spiritual future of the child because we know that there are events that seal the child's mentality. By teaching children during the first years of their lives, families play a crucial role in making certain children will be ready when they start going to school. Children learn behaviors through observations of family and society. If they see aggressive behavior, they learn aggressive behavior. If they see love and nurturing, that is what they learn. The family represents the primordial matrix of a human being's culture. Here is the place where the latent powers of the personal soul are awakened and developed. Family education does not just offer children academic guidance that involves their school-related work, but also more essentially offers extra-curricular assistance on social and cultural values taught by parents. Also, family education plays a crucial role in aiding the spiritual and moral development of the child and encouraging the eagerness to learn and natural curiosity of the child. Here is where the child becomes a small human being, from who later develops a great personality or a small delinquent."[143]

I had some great teachers in my small-town school. My first-grade teacher was Mrs. Mason, and she was wonderful. She pushed me to improve my reading skills and advance to an advanced reading group. For second grade I had Ms. Kirkpatrick. She was great too and had been by dad's second-grade teacher the first year she taught at my school. She was a stickler for discipline and pushed math skills. My third-grade teacher was Mrs. Cowden, also a wonderful teacher. She focused on reading. In her class we had to read books, stand in front of the class, and give a book report. My first book was the Hardy Boys, The Secret of The Caves.

Then there were the fourth, fifth, and sixth grades. The teachers were okay, but as I think back, they were average or a notch below. I say that because my fourth-grade teacher was more interested in finding a husband than in teaching (small town people tell everything about everyone). In the fifth grade all the boys needed to do to get good grades was to smile and wink at her (the teacher). My sixth-grade teacher was the first male teacher I had and was most interested in telling war stories. I learned later that he never served in the armed forces.

From the seventh grade on I had wonderful, caring teachers. Mr. Geheb for chemistry and physics, Mr. Adams and Mr. Wilcox for math, Mr. Berto for health & physical education as well as football coach, Mr. Buck and Mr. McCormick for speech and English, and Mr. Ebrite and Mr. Beach for industrial arts. At age 77 I still remember the impact each of them had on making me into what I am today. I also had a couple that

---

[143] Family's Roll in The Child's Education, Green, Emma, PregWorld, October 29, 2017.

were not so great. My Spanish teacher used the national (or maybe it was the state) proficiency test to prepare us for the proficiency test. We scored extremely high on the exam but have no idea how we actually compared with other students. Then there was my government teacher who, after I had spoken favorably about conservative political positions, pulled me aside after class and told me, "You are neither the smartest nor the dumbest student in class, but your political positions are stupid." Liberal politics were beginning to take hold in education back in the 1960s.

Another example is an experience with my son. He had a fabulous first-grade teacher. He was hospitalized and out of school for a couple of weeks. She visited him in the hospital, brought his lessons to us and after he returned to school spent extra time with him to be sure he was caught-up to the class. In his second-grade year the story was different. When my wife and I attended a parent-teacher conference, we were told that he was a discipline problem. When we asked for an explanation, we received the following example: "We had a fire drill, and when we re-entered the classroom, he turned the lights on. The first student back into the classroom was to turn the lights on and he was at the end of the line." I told her that did not sound like a discipline problem and that he probably just thought that since the first student in had not turned the lights on, he would turn them on. Her response was, "I do not want them to think, I just want them to do what they are told."

These personal stories are not unique at all. I would bet that nearly everyone has experience fabulous teachers, average teachers, and teachers, like my son's second grade teacher, that have no business in the classroom. Unfortunately, unions and tenure make it nearly impossible to clean the bottom-of-the barrel. I do not know for sure, but my guess is that my son's second grade teacher was a good, maybe even fabulous teacher early in her career, but lost it as the years passed. I have an older sister who taught mentally disabled children for more than 40 years. During that time, she was highly active with the teacher's union and a union leader at her school. It has been a decade or more ago that she and I were talking about the issues surrounding a teacher's strike and I told her I thought all the issues were only about improving things for teachers, but nothing about helping the students. She told me that I was right. She said that when she was working on union issues, they were sold under the guise of being for the students, but they were really about the teachers, not the students. More about the unions later.

Public school spending is at an all-time high. Max Eden reports that "Over the past half-century, America's per-pupil spending on K-12 education has nearly tripled, and, despite a dip from decreased tax revenues during the Great Recession, it now stands at an all-time high in most states."[144] He further states that "U.S. per-pupil expenditures have nearly tripled from $4,720 in 1966 to $13,847 (2018 dollars). America spends more per pupil than any other major developed nation – 10% more than the United Kingdom and 28% more than France. The typical private-sector worker experiences an 8% compensation increase when transitioning into education, while the typical teacher experiences a 3% salary decrease when transitioning into the private sector. Rising spending has not boosted teacher pay because the explosion in nonteaching staff has absorbed it instead; if the ratio of nonteaching staff to student enrollment had remained at its 1992 level, the money saved could have provided teachers with an additional $11,000 in compensation."[145] Most Americans believe that the U.S. spends too little on K-12 education. This misconception comes from the disconnect between political rhetoric and reality – thanks, Bernie Sanders and the liberal talking points.

Despite this spending, the U.S. students lag behind academically. Pew Research from 2017 found the "U.S. ranked 38th in math and 24th in science when compared against 71 other countries. Only two decades prior, the U.S.'s education system ranked 6th internationally.[146] In 2017-2018, the Adjusted Cohort Graduation Rate (ACGR) ranged from 69% in the District of Columbia to 91% in Iowa. The U.S. Average ACGR was 85%.[147]

---

[144] Issues 2020:Public School Spending Is at an All-Time High, Eden, Max, Manhattan Institute, July 25, 2019.

[145] Ibid.

[146] The US spends more on education than any other country, but students lag behind academically. Here's how much other countries spend and how well their students perform, DeGeruin, Mack, Insider, Auguse 22, 2019.

[147] U.S. Department of Education, National Center for Education Statistics. (2020). *The Condition of Education 2020* (NCES 2020-144, Public High School Graduation Rates.

It bothers me that 15% of high school students do not graduate, but what bothers me more is that high school graduation does not mean students are well educated. The U.S. ranking 38th in math and 24th in science does not speak well of what is happening in the classroom. From 2000 through 2004 I served as Director of Development at a community college. At that time, 70% of the high school graduates entering the college needed remedial education in math and English to prepare them for the college level courses.

Recently I have read that some schools are addressing inequities in math performance by keeping students who are at different skill levels in the same classroom (heterogeneous learning) for longer and not allowing pathways to fork in different directions until grades 11 and 12. Position papers by a national association for math educators' states that sorting advanced students into separate classes results in the over-representation of white and wealthy students. They say, "Those that have been privileged by the current system must be willing to give up that privilege for more equitable schooling."[148] So, equity is now more important than education? Schools must return to focusing on education, period. Adjusting curricula to affect social change is wrong. In a middle school in my community, teacher XX is promoting diversity awareness in her math classes with reading about historical Black figures and related fact sheets. I am not against students learning about successful Black figures, but with the U.S. ranking 38th in math, teacher XX needs to be fully focused on math.

When I was in the first grade we had three reading groups – red birds (best readers), blue birds (average readers), and yellow birds (slower readers). The teacher focused on the needs of each group. No way was she going to sacrifice the advancement of the best readers. Her goal was to help the blue birds and yellow birds move up a level – not hold the red birds back. I started as a blue bird but became a red bird in the second semester and it made me proud to do so.

I wrote earlier about the importance of the family in getting children off to a good start in school and in life. Now, President Biden wants to eliminate the "nuclear family" and place the government in charge of cradle-to-grave education. He starts with free universal pre-kindergarten

---

[148] No, Virginia isn't eliminating advanced courses. But some proposed changes are drawing fire., Gregory, Sara, The Virginia-Pilot, April 27, 2021.

for three and four year olds. According to him, this is to bring women back into the workforce. I have news for you, Mr. President, not all women want to be in the workplace, especially those with young children. Additionally, institutional childcare is not good for the kids. It is not that childcare is bad, some people need it, but the federal government pushing to get all children in childcare facilities is. According to J.D. Vance and Jenet Erickson, "Young children are clearly happier and healthier when they spend the day at home with a parent."[149]

In 1997 the provincial government of Quebec began offering childcare for 5 Canadian dollars a day to all families, regardless of income. Almost two decades later, economists Michael Baker, Kevin Milligan and Johathan Gruber found that "children from two-parent families who participated showed significant increases in anxiety, aggression and hyperactivity. Those effects persisted – and even grew – as they reached young adulthood. Self-reported health and life satisfaction decreased significantly. Boys who participated were more likely to commit crimes. It was, to put it bluntly, a disaster for Quebec's children."[150] Baker, Milligan, and Gruber continue saying, "A major longitudinal study conducted by the National Institute of Child Health and Human Development found that the more time infants and toddlers spent in nonfamilial care, the more likely they were to engage in aggressive, disobedient, or risky behavior.[151]

President Biden's "free" childcare program has nothing to do with putting women back into the workplace – it is a nice sounding "I'm giving you more 'free' stuff." The truth is, it is part of a well-orchestrated plan to get votes, take control of our children's education, and increase government's control over our lives.

I saw this tactic at work in Brazil. Luiz Inacia Lula da Silva served as president of Brazil from 2003 to 2011 – he was known as Lula. I was invited to lecture at the University of Taquari Valley (Univates) located in Lajeado, state of Rio Grande do Sul, Brazil. I, my wife, and a community college chancellor were there when Brazil held its national election in 2002. Lula was up for re-election, and he "guaranteed" his election by

---

[149] Biden's Daycare Plan Is Bad for Families, Vance, J.D. and Erickson, Jenet, Wall Street Journal, May 3, 2021.

[150] Ibid.

[151] Ibid.

dramatically reducing the price of bread and milk just prior to the election. The prices returned to "normal" after the election, but it shows that giving people something is how you win elections. It does not take voter fraud to win, just give stuff away. Sad!

A little side note here. Brazil's election was held on a Sunday and all adults were required to vote. The election officials guaranteed participation by requiring people to present certification of having voted to get their next paycheck. Additionally, the entire country counted and reported the votes, and announced the winner at 10:00 pm the day of the election. It is shameful what happened in Florida in 2000 and Pennsylvania, Georgia, New York, and other states in 2020. More on that in the chapter on election integrity.

I am genuinely concerned that teachers' unions, in addition to working for teachers, are driving school curricula. According to The Center for Responsive Politics, in 2020, the teachers' unions gave $86,586,993 to Democrats and $3,551,686 to Republicans. With such staunch support for the far-left political movement, it is not surprising that schools are teaching Critical Race Theory and Equity in the classrooms.

Britannica defines Critical Race Theory as an "intellectual movement and loosely organized framework of legal analysis based on the premise that race is not a natural, biologically grounded feature of physically distinct subgroups of human beings but a socially constructed (culturally invented) category that is used to oppress and exploit people of color. Critical race theorists hold that the law and legal institutions in the United States are inherently racist insofar as they function to create and maintain social, economic, and political inequalities between whites and nonwhites, especially African Americans."[152]

Kimberle Crenshaw, a founding critical race theorist and a law professor at UCLA and Columbia universities, defines critical race like this: "Critical race theory is a practice. It's an approach to grappling with a history of White supremacy that rejects the belief that what's in the past is in the past, and that the laws and systems that grow from the past are detached from it."[153]

---

[152] Britannica.com, Critical Race Theory, updated April 2, 2021.
[153] What critical race theory is – and isn't, Karimi, Faith, CNN, October 1, 2020.

The theory grew from activists and scholars in the 1970s as a reaction to the perceived slowing of progress of the civil rights movement. I have a different take on it. Critical race theory fits perfectly into the Marxist playbook dividing people. In short, it teaches people to hate each other. Teaching people to hate has no place in our educational system! The three "Rs" are no longer readin, ritin, and rithmetic – now they are readin (what leftists say you can read), ritin (what leftist say you can write), and racism (and the leftists blame racism for all the country's ills)!

States need to follow the example of Idaho governor Brad Little who signed bill H 377 into law on April 28, 2021. The bill prevents teachers from "indoctrinating" students into belief systems that claim that members of any race, sex, religion, ethnicity, or national origin are inferior or superior to other groups. The bill also makes it illegal to make students "affirm, adopt or adhere to beliefs that members of these groups are today responsible for past actions of the groups to which they claim to belong.[154]

Pushing 'equity' over 'equality' adds to the critical race theory. John Leonard says, "*Equality* means treating everyone with fairness. In a society governed by the principles of equality, every citizen has the same, or equal, opportunity to achieve success regardless of age, gender, race, religion, political affiliation, or any other reason, save for the limitations of that individual's qualifications and abilities."[155]

Leonard uses Barack Obama and Richard Montanez to prove the United States provided equal opportunity for literally anyone with initiative. Leonard writes, "We all know Barack Obama came from humble origins in Hawaii to become the first black president in U.S. history... Obama has managed to rake in tens of millions of dollars for 'writing' an absurd number of memoirs for a man who has accomplished remarkably little in his life.

But who the heck is Richard Montanez? The former janitor mopping the floors at the Frito Lay factory in Rancho Cucamonga, California was only earning four bucks an hour plus benefits when he pitched the idea of Flaming Hot Cheetos to Pepsi CEO Roger Enrico, a marketing concept

---

[154] Idaho governor signs bill to ban critical race theory from being taught in schools, Jordan, Mike, The Guardian, May 6, 2021.
[155] Equality vs. Equity in Joe Biden's America, Leonard, John, American Thinker, December 25, 2020.

that earned billions of dollars profits. Obama received his juris doctor degree from Harvard, while Montanez jokes that he earned a PhD from being poor, hungry, and determined...his net worth today is estimated between $14 and $15 million, and Montanez is currently CEO of the Cheetos brand. Not bad for a former janitor, right?"[156]

Put simply, equity is ownership. If your home is worth $100,000 and you owe the bank $75,000, you have $25,000 equity in the house. In other words, you own 25% of the house and the bank owns 75% of it. Equity is a financial term.

The liberals are exploiting the fact that the words sound similar and are using it to push a redistribution of wealth agenda. They do not want equal opportunity; they want equal outcomes. They want to take resources from one group and give those resources to another group. It is the redistribution of resources (our hard earned wealth).

When applied to education, Jennifer Kabbany writes, "Leftist diversity educators insist equality is unfair and push equity as the solution. It's an insidious curriculum that dumbs down education, installs quotas, and advances a socialist agenda.[157]

Jordan Peterson says, "There is simply no excuse for this doctrine [equity]. First, it suffers from the oversimplification typical of ideological thinkers: that one cause (prejudice) is sufficient explanation for a very complex phenomenon (that of inequality, which is a far deeper problem that can be laid at the feet of inefficient social organization). Second, it is impossible to implement, as there are simply too many...of the identity group sort to possibly treat in the 'equitable' manner demanded by the ideologues. Finally, it is being forcibly instituted by individuals for whom the hypothesis that the West is a singularly oppressive patriarchy is an unshakeable axiom..."[158]

The COVID-19 pandemic has been a catastrophe for millions of students. In 2019, 56.6 million students attended elementary and secondary school in the United States. Those students were enrolled in approximately 131,000 schools, most of which were closed - closed for legitimate reasons

---

[156] Ibid.

[157] Equality versus equity, Kabbany, Jennifer, The College Fix, May 4, 2021.

[158] Jordan Peterson: The Dangerous Doctrine of Equity, Peterson, Jordan B., Sovereign Nation, August 26, 2019.

the first few weeks but kept closed through the actions of the teachers' unions.

Jason Riley reports about COVID-19 that, "We've known from the earliest days of the virus that youngsters are the least likely to catch it or spread it to others. We also know that many low-income parents struggle with home schooling and need to go back to work. Distance learning exacerbates racial and economic achievement gaps and takes a heavy psychological toll on kids. Union leaders could not care less. The teachers' unions have used the pandemic to demand more money and more-generous benefits. The United Teachers of Los Angeles requested free childcare for its members as a condition for returning to the classroom. The Covid-relief law President Biden signed in March allocates $123 billion for public schools, with no requirement that districts first reopen for in-person learning to receive the money. What Americans have learned from the lockdowns is the degree to which unions control not only the public-school systems but by extension the everyday lives of tens of millions of parents with school-age children."[159]

The Wall Street Journal editorial board reports that the "American Federation of Teachers chief Randi Weingarten gets the CDC to change its school opening guidance. In early February 2021, new CDC Director Rochelle Walensky told reporters in a press conference that 'schools can safely reopen, and that safe reopening does not suggest that teachers need to be vaccinated.' Oops. She forgot to consult the expert opinion of Ms. Weingarten, a major supporter of President Biden. After unions howled... the CDC rolled out official school reopening guidelines that recommended teachers be given 'high priority' for vaccines and curiously echoed other union demands."[160]

Patrick O'Donnell describes how two schools in Ohio have stayed open through the pandemic. He reports that, "Staff at St. Stanislaus elementary school in Cleveland have spent the school year constantly reminding students to keep masks up over noses, to keep safe distance, and sanitizing everything, including the Easter eggs given to the youngest

---

[159] Teachers Unions' Covid Cop-Outs Are a Winning Issue for GOP, Riley, Jason L., The Wall Street Journal, May 4, 2021.
[160] The Centers for Politics and Unions, The Editorial Board, The Wall Street Journal, May 4, 2021.

students."[161] O'Donnell continues saying that about two thirds of the high-poverty, high-minority students at St. Stanislaus are coming to school every day. Principal Deborah Martin said, "We had zero student cases. Zero teacher cases. Zero."[162]

Arian Campo-Flores reports that, "As districts around the U.S. continue to grapple with whether to reopen classrooms amid the coronavirus pandemic, data show Florida started in-person learning without turning schools into superspreaders. The state was one of the earliest to resume in-person instruction in August, following an executive order by Education Commissioner Richard Corcoran that directed districts to provide families the option of classroom learning five days a week or risk losing funding. In the seven months since, Florida schools have avoided major outbreaks of Covid-19 and maintained case rates lower than those in the wider community. Mr. Corcoran said 80% of students in Florida are now attending schools in-person full – or part-time.[163]

Michael Birnbaum reports, "Most of Europe kept schools open even during a worst-on-the-planet second wave of infections this fall. And still, schools appear to be relatively safe environments, public health officials say. As long as they adhered to a now-established set of precautions – mask-wearing, hand-washing, ventilation – schools are thought to have played only a limited role in accelerating coronavirus transmission in Europe. 'It is still difficult for me to understand why school are closed in the United States,' said Otto Helve, a specialist in pediatric infectious diseases at the Finnish Institute for Health and Welfare who has studied coronavirus transmission in schools. 'Schools are not driving the epidemic.'"[164]

Parents need to control their children's education – not big government, Dr. Fauci, Dr. Birx, President Biden or the teachers' unions.

I mentioned earlier in this chapter that I had some particularly good teachers, and I was taught to love America. My first and third grade

---

[161] How 2 Schools in Ohio Have Stayed Open (and Safe) Through the Pandemic, O'Donnell, Patrick, T74 Newsletter, April 14, 2021.

[162] Ibid.

[163] Florida Schools Reopened Without Becoming Covid-19 Superspreaders, Campo-Flores, Arian, The Wall Street Journal, March 17, 2021.

[164] Europe's school still open, still relatively safe, through covid-19 second wave, Birnbaum, Michael, The Washington Post, December 1, 2020.

teachers had lost their husbands in WWII and some of my high school teachers had served in the war. In grammar school we started each day with the Pledge of Allegiance. I remember when "under God" was added to the Pledge in 1954. Those were the days before teachers' unions had as much power as they do today. The local teachers, parents, and school boards ran the schools without interference from the unions.

The unions were around, but they were still fledglings. According to the Hechinger Report, The National Education Association (NEA) was formed in 1857 by 43 educators. The Chicago Teachers Federation was formed in 1871 to raise teacher salaries and pensions. The American Federation of Teachers was formed in Chicago in 1916, but it was not until 1959 when Wisconsin became the first state to pass a collective bargaining law for public employees. As other states followed, union membership, and strength, increased.

It has been many years since I had children in school, but in 1985 (give or take a year), when my son was in high school, I served on textbook selection committees for math and history. When reviewing the history textbooks, I was reminded of how old I was when I saw that the history in the last half or more of the new texts covered what I had studied as current events. I do not remember seeing any anti-American history in any of the books. For math, I was extremely impressed with the head of the math department, unfortunately I do not remember his name. We had narrowed the texts down to two good books and I was asked which one I preferred. I responded that I preferred textbook "A" because as a parent, I am frequently asked for some help with homework. Textbook "A" was written in a manner that would make it quite easy for me to quickly review the lesson and provide the help needed. The other parents agreed. One of the teachers, however, said he wanted textbook "B" because it came complete with homework assignments, worksheets, and tests. The department head responded to him with something like, "The job of the teacher is to tailor the homework assignments, worksheets, and tests to each class. We are going to select textbook "A." I wonder if that is about when some teachers began thinking about themselves more than the students.

Unions have enormous influence over the public schools but not much over the private and charter schools. The Wall Street Journal editorial board writes, "Ten years ago in these columns we hailed Indiana for its leadership in establishing one of America's most ambitious school voucher programs. On Thursday, the Indiana Legislature built on that achievement by approving a budget that will take the program to 48,000 students a year from about 37,000.

The choice provisions in the budget have three main components. The first would lift the income cap for eligibility to $145,000 from $96,000. This would make as much as 90% of the population eligible for the program. The bill would also increase the voucher amount to 90% of tuition support levels. Another provision would establish Education Savings Accounts for children with special needs. The budget also increases the per student grants for charter schools. The teachers' unions are unhappy. Their beef is that money to expand choice is taken from traditional public schools. And this year they lobbied school boards to pass resolutions opposed to school choice."[165]

Paul Peterson reports that the lockdowns give school choice a boost. A third of U.S. students still are not going to a classroom every day. Many urban districts open their doors only to young children or for just two days a week. Peterson continues, "School-choice advocates have scored big victories around the country. Indiana enlarged its voucher program. Montana lifted caps on charter schools. Arkansas now offers tax-credit scholarship to low-income students. West Virginia and Kentucky have funded savings accounts to help parents pay tuition at private schools. Florida has enlarged its tax-credit scholarship programs. Even Rhode Island Governor Dan McKee promises to veto a moratorium on new charter schools."[166] The public schools have failed our students during the pandemic and U.S. students lag behind students from other countries.

In 2019, Kate Barrington, claimed that "The results of a new study show that private school education may be no better than public school education."[167] However, Hudson Lindenberger states that, "A recent recap of high school graduates showed private school students scoring 4 points

[165] Hoosiers Lead the Voucher Way, The Editorial Board, The Wall Street Journal, April 22, 2021.

[166] Lockdown Give School Choice a Boost, Peterson, Paul E., Wall Street Journal, April 28, 2021.

[167] New Study Confirms That Private Schools Are No Better Than Public Schools, Barrington, Kate, Public School Review, March 20, 2019.

higher on the ACT test. The same disparity is found between primary and middle schools, according to the NCES (National Center for Education Statistics). A comparison of mathematics tests showed private schools scored 18 points higher for eighth graders and 8 points higher for fourth graders. Reading had the same results, with private schools outscoring their public counterparts by 18 points in eighth grade and 15 points in fourth grade."[168]

Whether a student will be better off in a private school or a public school depends on where they live and the schools in their district. We are fortunate in my community to have good public schools and good private schools for parents and students to choose from. Unfortunately, some public schools, especially those in low-income, inner-city locations, are not as good as others. Regardless, every parent should have a choice as to the school their child attends.

Teacher unions are against private and charter schools for one, or both, of two reasons. It is all about money, or they know they cannot successfully compete with the private sector schools.

In Catholicism, subsidiarity is an organizing principle that matters ought to be handled by the smallest, lowest or least centralized competent authority. Political decisions should be taken at local level, if possible, rather than by a central authority. This principle applies to a myriad of things, but especially to education. With that in mind, I pose the question, do we need the Department of Education?

On October 28, 2011, Charles Murray delivered a speech at a conference on "Markets, Government, and Common Good" in Atlanta, Georgia. The following are quotes are from that speech: "1) Is the Department of Education constitutional? At the time the Constitution was written, education was not even considered a function of local government, let alone the federal government. Article 1, Section 8 of the Constitution enumerates the things over which Congress has the power to legislate. Not only does the list not include education, there is no plausible rationale for squeezing education in under the commerce clause. I'm sure the Supreme Court found a rationale, but it could not have been plausible."[169] Murray

---

[168] Private School vs. Public School: Facts, Benefits & Statistics, Hindenberger, Hudson, Love & Money / Education, April 22, 2021.

[169] imprints.hillsdale.edu/do-we-need-the-department-of-education/.

stated he is in favor of abolishing the Department of Education but acknowledges he is in a small minority on that point.

Murray also addresses a pragmatic question. "2) Are there serious problems in education that can be solved only at the federal level? The first major federal spending on education was triggered by the launch of the first space satellite, Sputnik, in the fall of 1957, which created a perception that the United States had fallen behind the Soviet Union in science and technology. The National Defense Education Act of 1958 was specifically designed to encourage more students to go into math and science. When the push for President Johnson's Great Society programs began in the mid-1960s, it was inevitable that the federal government would attempt to reduce black-white disparities, and it did so in 1965 with two landmark bills – the Elementary and Secondary Education Act and the Higher Education Act."[170]

The Department of Education did not come into being until 1980, but large-scale involvement of the federal government in education dates from 1965. Murray continues, "3) So what is the federal government's track record in education?"[171] Citing trend data of the National Assessment of Educational Progress (NAEP), Murray continues, "Consider, for instance, the results for the math test for students in fourth, eighth and twelfth grades from 1978 through 2004. The good news is that the scores for fourth graders showed significant improvement in both reading and math. The bad news is that the baseline year of 1978 represents the nadir [the lowest point] of the test score decline from the mid-1960s through the 1970s. Probably we are today about where we were in math achievement in the 1960s. For reading, the story is even bleaker...The overall data on the performance of K-12 students give no reason to think the federal involvement, which took the form of the Department of Education after 1979, has been an engine of improvement. If the Department of Education disappeared from next year's budget, would anyone notice? The only reason that anyone would notice is the money. Sadly, the education lobby will prevent any serious inroads on the Department of Education for the foreseeable future."[172]

---

[170] Ibid.

[171] Ibid.

[172] Ibid.

If President Biden does not continue Donald Trump's attempts to transform the Federal role in education, there is no hope to return to the principle of subsidiarity. The government fiscal year is October 1 of one calendar year through September 30 of the next year. President Trump's 2021 budget request for the Department of Education marked a significant expansion of his effort to transform the Federal role in education. His 2021 request consolidates most Federal elementary and secondary education programs into flexible block grants that allow States to decide how best to use Federal funds to meet the needs of their students and improve workforce preparation. His support for a Federal tax-credit for voluntary donations to State-identified scholarship programs makes money available for a wide range of public and private programs, including private schools. There are many elements of his program that counter government overreach by returning K-12 educational decisions block to where the belong – at the state and local level.

There are other educational issues to be addressed and I will include abbreviated comments on some of those in the chapter entitled, "Miscellaneous."

ACTIONS

1. E pluribus unum is Latin for "Out of many, one." It was the de facto motto of the United States until the Congress adopted "In God We Trust" as the official motto in 1956. Fight to make our country "One" again by eliminating "Cancel Culture," "White Supremacy," and "Equity" from your schools' curriculum.
2. Insist on having History and Civics education that promote unity – not division.
3. Insist that school board members have a child or grandchild in the school systeem.
4. Attend school board meetings and "raise hell" when board members disregard what the parents believe is best for their students.
5. Work to promote family involvement in education by working to form strong family, school, and community partnerships.

6. Assure your school has, and enforces, a schoolwide discipline plan that is applied fairly and consistently.
7. Assure your community has Alternative Education options for disruptive students.
8. Do not allow the "dumbing down" of your schools' student population.
9. Eliminate Common Core.
10. Mandate homework for students. (More on that in Miscellaneous)
11. Assure that critical race theory is not taught in your schools.
12. Insist that your schools educate children, not politicize or indoctrinate them.
13. Acknowledge that a child's first teachers are his parents, not school labor unions, school boards, or the Department of Education.

CHAPTER THIRTEEN

Miscellaneous

Before I go to my closing chapter on election integrity, there are some subjects I want to address that deserve a full chapter but would result in a never-ending book. There are other subjects that will require only a few lines or paragraphs, but everyone needs to consider.

Homework

I included "Mandate homework" in my actions for education. This recommendation comes from a personal experience in 1961. I was a Freshman at Purdue University and during one of my breaks, I visited my brother-in-law's school where he taught English and Music. My visit was on a Monday and before classes started, the teachers held a meeting to decide which teacher could give 20 minutes of homework on Monday, Tuesday, Wednesday, and Thursday. The school board declared that students could not be given more than a total of 20 minutes of homework on any day, Monday through Thursday, and no homework on Friday or over the weekend. The parents did not want homework on weekends because it would interfere with Junior Country Club activities. The school board followed the demands of the parents, but the parents' demands were wrong. They placed Junior Country Club activities above the education of their children. Please do not follow the example of those parents!

When I was in school, I had homework every day including weekends. Homework helped to cement what I had learned and when I needed some help from my parents, it kept them up to date on what I was being taught.

Hugs are Important

I could have put this experience in the part of the 'education' chapter when talking about the importance of family, but it is more than education. It is about a person's sense of self-worth, of belonging, of being safe, and being loved.

Ray Williams gives eight reasons why we need human touch:[173]

- "Decreased violence. Less touch as a child leads to greater violence. Child developmental research illustrates that the absence of physical bonding and healthy attachment between an adult and child may result in lifelong emotional disturbances.

- Greater trust between individuals. Daniel Keltner cites the work of neuroscientist Edmund Ross, who found that physical touch activates the brain's orbitofrontal cortex, linked to feelings of reward and compassion.

- Economic Gain. Keltner links economic benefits to physical touch, probably because 'touch signals safety and trust; it soothes.'

- Decreased disease and stronger immune system. According to research conducted at the University of North Carolina, women who receive more hugs from their partners have lower heart rates and blood pressure. Hugs strengthen the immune system...by stimulating the thymus gland, which regulates and balances the body's production of white blood cells, which keeps you healthy and disease free.

- Stronger team dynamics. Paul Zak argues that hugs or handshakes are likely to cause the release of the neurochemical oxytocin, which increases the chances that a person will treat you 'like family,' even if you just met.

---

[173] 8 Reasons Why We Need Human Touch More Than Ever, Williams, Ray, Wired for Success, March 20, 2015.

- More non-sexual emotional intimacy. A study showed that two-thirds of women agreed to dance with a man who touched her on the arm a second or two before making the ask.
- Greater learning engagement. When teachers touch students platonically, it encourages their learning. When librarians pat the hand of a student checking out a book, that student says he or she likes the library more and is likely to return.
- Overall wellbeing. Adults require human touch to thrive. Research is suggesting that touch is truly fundamental to human communication, bonding, and health."

It was 1996 or 1997 when my wife and I were playing Mr. & Mrs. Santa Clause at a local department store. The store had shopping hours for the residents of nursing homes and assisted living facilities. The shoppers loved having their pictures taken with Mr. & Mrs. Clause. The store invited the junior high school choir from a local school to sing Christmas carols and other songs to entertain the shoppers. At the end of the choir's performance, they lined up to get a candy cane from Santa Clause. A few kids came through the line and took their candy and then a girl came to Santa and said, "I don't want a candy cane. I want a hug!" My heart broke as I gave her a hug. As the other kids came through the line none of them wanted a candy cane, they all wanted a hug. Today, I could not give those kids hugs without being accused of being a pedophile.

Children being starved for hugs is unbelievably cruel. Is this because the family unit is being dissolved? Is it the preoccupation with digital media?

Life Without Electricity

The May 2021 cyberattack on the Colonial Pipeline demonstrated how crippling an interruption to our fuel delivery system can be. The 5,500-mile pipeline carries refined gasoline and jet fuel from Texas up the East Coast to New York. The pipeline carries 45% of the East Coast's fuel and it was forced to shut down after being attacked by the DarkSide ransomware gang. The pipeline was down for six-days and long lines at gas stations were reminiscent of the gas shortage of the 1970s during the Carter administration. The Colonial Pipeline shutdown forced airplanes to add fueling stops to their flights because of the jet fuel shortage. People were even seen putting gasoline into plastic bags and thousands of gas stations were out of gas.

Gasoline shortages are certainly disruptive and inconvenient but not crippling. Colonial Pipeline paid a $5 million ransom to reopen the pipeline, so it is reasonable to assume that ransomware groups will continue to attack our infrastructure. What if the next attack is on our electrical grid? The grid is vulnerable to geomagnetic storms generated by solar activity, electromagnetic pulses (EMP) produced by high altitude nuclear detonations, cyberattacks, and physical attack.[174]

Matthew Weiss reports that high voltage (HV) transformers, "are the weak link in the system, and the Federal Energy Regulatory Commission (FERC) has identified 30 of these as being critical. The simultaneous loss of just 9, in various combinations, could cripple the network and lead to a cascading failure, resulting in a 'coast-to-coast blackout.'"[175]

If these transformers are irreparably damaged there is sizeable question whether they can be replaced. It takes 12-24 months to manufacture one domestically, but 85% are manufactured overseas and take about 3 years to produce. They are also expensive at $10 million each.

The grid could be 'hardened' against solar activity, but that has not been done. An EMP could be delivered by a terrorist group supported by an America-hating country like Iran and cyberattacks and physical attacks could be delivered by many countries and groups.

Alan Urban reports that, "An EMP strike that wipes out electricity across the nations would ultimately lead to the demise of up to 90% of the population."[176] This would occur within a year or so. Whether a major blackout is nationwide or concentrated in a large section of the country, life would certainly change, especially if the outage is of long duration. No

---

[174] Energy, Sustainability and Society, An assessment of threats to the American power grid, Energy, Sustainability and Society, Weiss, Matthew & Weiss, Martin, Biomed Central, May 29, 2019.

[175] ibid.

[176] Why 90% of the Population Would Die Without Electricity, Urban, Alan, Urban Survival Site, September 18, 2017.

electricity means no water – it takes electricity to pump water. Sanitation systems run on electricity. Most people rely on grocery stores for food – but without electricity it is likely that stores would be looted. Refrigeration would stop working as would climate control. Loss of heat in the coldest climates would result in unimaginable deaths. How long would it take to collapse into chaos - a few days, a month?

I do not think I am an alarmist, but maybe I am. Discussions about the cataclysmic outcome of a nationwide power outage have been occurring for decades, but nothing has been done about it. President Biden's $2.2 trillion infrastructure plan, officially the American Jobs Plan, has $518 billion, 24% of the plan cost, dedicated to bridges, highways, roads, ports, waterways, airports, high-speed broadband Internet, modernizing the electric grid, and improving infrastructure resilience.[177] The plan calls for $400 billion to raise pay for home care workers, $300 billion in aid to manufacturers and businesses regardless of any connection to infrastructure, incentives for the purchase of electric vehicles, and $100 billion for public schools.

Most of the money devoted to the electric grid goes toward his goal of producing 100% carbon-free electricity by 2035. Seems to me that securing the grid from EMF, cyber and physical attacks should be of high priority. We need an infrastructure bill, but it needs to be a clean bill free of political pet projects like the push to unionize the American workforce. Remove the $1.6 trillion of pet project spending and add some of it back to real infrastructure.

American Families Plan

President Biden's $1.8 trillion American Families Plan is an effort to expand federal government control over some of the most personal aspects of family life.[178] According to Fishpaw, et al., the new childcare spending plan would create, "a one-size-fits-all government program that would be

---

[177] How much infrastructure is in Biden's infrastructure plan, Colvin, Geoff, Fortune, April 6, 2021.

[178] 5 Things You Need to Know About Biden's $1.8 Trillion American Families Plan, Fishpaw, Marie / Burke, Lindsay / Badger, Doug / Dickerson, Matthew / Ford, Leslie / Greszler, Rachel / Rector, Robert, The Daily Signal, May 10, 2021.

restrictive, unresponsive, and less generous than existing employer-provided programs. At the same time...the proposal encourages parents not to stay home with their children by favoring center-based and government-run pre-kindergarten over family care. Such policies prioritize maximizing tax revenues and measured economic output by having all parents work full time while growing the government's involvement in raising children."[179]

The plan spends $200 billion on "free" universal preschool for 3 and 4-year-olds, based on the premise that children benefit academically from preschool. Fishpaw continues, "However, the most rigorous research shows that government preschool programs [Head Start, for example] consistently fail to produce any sustained benefits for children and actually have some negative effects."[180] According to Fishpaw, the Plan would make permanent a $40 billion expansion of Obamacare that, "could threaten employer-sponsored coverage for millions of Americans, forcing them into Affordable Care Act plans that generally have narrower networks, higher cost-sharing, and higher deductibles than their job-based plans."[181] Fishpaw also says the Plan is a permanent expansion of the Welfare state and increase taxes that hurt families. "The plan would increase the tax burden on property left by deceased relatives to the next generation."[182] Do you remember when children inheriting a farm or business from a parent had to sell the farm or business to pay the inheritance tax? We could be headed right back there.

COVID-19 Relief Bill

Promoted as "the COVID-19 Relief Bill," the legislation is actually the $1.9 trillion "American Rescue Plan" that has little to do with COVID-19. My assessment is that the Bill was well received by the public because it was another money give away. Giving money away is always a sure way for politicians to get voters to 'like' them. Individuals with an adjusted gross

---

[179] ibid.
[180] ibid.
[181] ibid.
[182] ibid.

income of $75,000 or less, and married couples with adjusted gross income of $150,000 or less received $1,400 per individual.

Thanks to the COVID-19 relief bill, 39 million households will get up to $3,600 stimulus in monthly payments. Greg Dawson reports that, "In the latest evolution of creeping Universal Basic Income, Biden administration officials said on May 17, 2021, that a poverty-fighting measure included in the COVID-19 relief bill will deliver monthly payments to households including 88% of children in the United States, starting in July."[183] The Treasury and the IRS announced Eligible families will receive up to $300 per month for each child under age 6 and up to $250 per month for each child aged 6 and above. The credit will phase out when incomes exceed $150,000 for a household or $75,000 for individuals.

Matthew D. Dickerson reports that the relief bill, "is stuffed with a wish list of progressive policies that have nothing to do with the pandemic. For example, nearly $90 billion is earmarked for a taxpayer-funded bailout of union pension plans. This union bailout gets about twice as much funding as COVID-19 testing and contact tracing."[184] Dickerson continues with information about the $126 billion for K-12 schools. "The non-partisan Congressional Budget Office says that only $6.2 billion of that – just five percent – would actually be spent by October. More of this funding will be spent in 2026 than in 2021."[185]

The only things the bill should have addressed: bringing the spread of the disease under control and getting the country back to pre-Covid social and economic conditions.

Inflation

We all know what inflation is – it is when something you bought last month for a dollar now costs a dollar and ten cents. Year to date price increases reported by FOX News on May 19, 2021, include the following:

---

[183] 39 Million Households To Get Up To $3,600 Stimulus in Monthly Payments, Dawson, Greg, True Conservative HUB, May 18, 2021.
[184] Joe Biden's Coronavirus Stimulus Bill: A $1.9 Trillion Disaster, Dickerson, Matthew D., The Heritage Foundation, March 11, 2021.
[185] ibid.

- Dining Out – Up 3.7%
- Pork – Up 59%
- Wheat – Up 21%
- Gasoline – Up from $2.40 a gallon to $3.05 a gallon
- Food Prices – Up 3.5%
- Lumber – Up 250%
- Housing – Up 11%
- New Cars – Up 9%
- Household Items (general merchandise) - Up 5.2-7.2%

So, what is happening that everything is costing more today than it did a few months ago? I am not an economist, and do not pretend to understand all the nuances of microeconomics and macroeconomics, so this is going to be extremely basic.

When the government prints more money, like to cover the $6 trillion in passed and proposed spending (put forth in January 2021) with only $2.1 trillion in tax revenues, each dollar is worth a little less. Think of it as the dollar shrinking and getting smaller. It takes more 'smaller' dollars to buy something than it did when the dollar was 'bigger.'

When the price of oil increases, heating bills go up, the cost of gasoline, jet fuel, and other items produced from oil go up. The cost of transportation goes up and that cost is passed on to consumers through price increases.

When wages go up, employers must cover that cost by doing one of two things – increase the price of goods and services or decrease the number of employees using automation. For many small businesses, automation is not an option and if they increase prices too much, they cannot compete with the larger employers. Their other option – go out of business.

When the demand is greater than the supply, prices increase. That is one of the factors now increasing the price of lumber and pork.

When taxes on businesses go up, those tax increases are passed on to the consumer in the form of higher prices. Same with tariffs that increase the price of imported goods.

The bottom line, inflation is a tax on everyone, and it hurts the lower income families the most.

Incentives Pay More Than Work

The COVID-19 stimulus bill provides a $300 a week in extra jobless benefits until September 2021. The extra benefit may have been necessary during the height of the COVID-19 pandemic, but I must question whether it is necessary now.

The May 11, 2021, Bureau of Labor Statistics reported 8.1 million job openings in March. The Wall Street Journal reports that "Overall job openings in March increased by about 600,000 while new hires ticked up a mere 200,000. The number of workers who quit their jobs also grew by 125,000. This is usually a sign of a strengthening labor market, but in this case some quitters may be leaving their jobs because they figure then can make more unemployed for the next six months."[186]

Several states, including Florida, Montana, North Carolina, and Indiana, have tightened requirements to receive unemployment benefits and have stopped payments to people who turn work down. The Wall Street Journal reports that "Montana already offers a maximum individual unemployment benefit of $572 a week, and with the federal bonus the jobless can collect the equivalent of up to $21.80 an hour for doing nothing. That translates into an annual income of $45,344 for a single worker and $90,688 for a household with two workers on welfare. With state and federal benefits combined, about half of Montana's workers make more than their prior earnings while unemployed."[187] Indiana has a maximum unemployment payment of $390 a week, according to the state Department of Workforce Development. The $300 federal bonus increases that to $690 a week or $17.25 an hour.

There is a legitimate purpose for unemployment benefits and there are many people who need it as a bridge between a lost job and finding new work. However, there are also many that are too willing to take the easy way out and get paid for doing nothing. This applies to some high-income workers as well as lower wage earners. For example, my wife and I had an acquaintance who was a nurse working as a visiting nurse. She lost her job

---

[186] A Jolt for White House Economists, The Editorial Board, The Wall Street Journal, May 14, 2021.
[187] Monta to Feds: No More No-Work Bonus, The Editorial Board, The Wall Street Journal, May 4, 2021.

because the company she worked for closed its local office. Even though hospitals at the time were desperate for nurses, she said, "I'll just collect unemployment until it runs out and then get a new job."

Let us stop paying people more to do nothing than what they can make working.

Gun Control

Liberals and conservatives view the Second Amendment differently – very differently. The issue of gun control surfaces whenever there is a mass shooting. On Tuesday, March 23, 2021, President Biden commented on the March 22nd shooting at a Colorado grocery store that killed 10, including one police officer. Biden said, "I don't need to wait another minute, let alone an hour, to take commonsense steps that will save lives in the future. This is not and should not be a partisan issue. It is an American issue."[188] Conservatives strongly believe in the Second Amendment that guarantees the right of citizens to own guns.

In 2008, the US Supreme Court ruled in District of Columbia v. Heller the federal government could not strip citizens of their rights to own handguns for self-defense. Don Purdum states, "It's settled law that Americans have the right to own firearms to protect themselves, the Supreme Court only delt with handguns."[189]

Purdum continues, "When the US Constitution was ratified in 1787, there was an agreed-upon societal view that people should protect themselves from the government when it gets out of control...Access to guns was an absolute necessity to ensure the government did not violate people's liberties. Fear of tyranny at the time was real and legitimate."[190]

Many argue that today's America is different and that the 1787 need for people to possess firearms no longer exist. I wholeheartedly disagree. Susanne Edward reports that, "Right now, just three countries on the

---

[188] Biden urges gun reform after Colorado shooting: 'Don't wait another minute,' McCarthy, Tom, Greve, Joan E, and Walters, Joanna, The Guardian, March 23, 2021.

[189] https://www.rightwing.org/republicans-gearing-up-to-protect-2...m=email& utm-campaign=newsletter&utm-content=RWnewsletter.

[190] Ibid.

planet mention the right to own arms in their constitutions: The United States, Mexico, and Guatemala. The latter two, however, have chipped away at their constitutional rights so much they've been reduced to almost no right at all. But it is important to note that, not so long ago, there were six other nations that had the right to own a gun. In 2019 the *New York Times* reported that Bolivia, Costa Rica, Columbia, Honduras, Nicaragua, and Liberia all had protections inspired by the Second Amendment of the U.S. Bill of Rights, but that those six nations had all mostly eradicated this fundamental right."[191] Edward further reports that the crackdown in Bolivia was sold under the auspices of stopping arms trafficking. Bolivia's actions inspired Venezuela's crusade against civilian gun ownership. Costa Rican reforms began with listing contraband weapons that included semi-automatic long arms, magazine capacities of more than ten rounds, and any weapon classified as mass destruction. Columbia implemented a nationwide injunction against the carrying of firearms. Gun control efforts in Honduras have been "largely ineffective because the government cannot issue force over the criminal groups."[192] After sweeping firearms regulations in Nicaragua, protesters of President Daniel Ortega were met with gunfire and hundreds lost their lives. In Liberia, "No individual, group, organization or entity other than the Government of Liberia may own, possess or cause to be brought into Liberia any firearm of any type."[193]

The right to bear arms in those countries did not happen overnight. They were chipped away a little bit at a time. The movement to "chip away" gun rights in America is highly likely to gain strength in 2021. The Biden-Harris Administration has announced six initial actions to address the "gun violence public health epidemic."[194] According to the White House statement, "last month (March 2021), a bipartisan coalition in the House passed two bills to close loopholes in the gun background check system. Congress should close those loopholes and go further, including closing "boyfriend" and stalking loopholes that currently allow people

---

[191] When Rights Are Surrendered, Edward, Susanne, America's 1st FREEDOM, April 2021.
[192] Ibid.
[193] Ibid.
[194] FACT SHEET: Biden-Haris Administration Announces Initial Actions to Address the Gun Violence Public Health Epidemic, whitehouse.gov., April 7, 2021.

found by the courts to be abusers to possess firearms, banning assault weapons and high-capacity magazines, repealing gun manufacturers' immunity from liability, and investing in evidence-based community violence interventions. Congress should also pass an appropriate national "red flag" law (explained below)."[195]

Not willing to wait for Congress to act, The Justice Department stated it will issue proposed rules to help stop the proliferation of "ghost guns (gun kits)," make clear when a device marketed as a stabilizing brace effectively turns a piston into a short-barreled rifle and will propose model "red flag" legislation.

Books have been written about gun control and if you want to read in depth positions on the issues here are some suggestions: Gunfight: The Battle Over the Right to Bear Arms in America by Adam Winkler; The Second Amendment by Michael Waldman; The Politics of Gun Control by Robert Spitzer; More Guns, Less Crime by John R. Lott, Jr.; The Gun Debate by Kristin Goss and Phillip J. Cook; and Control: Exposing the Truth About Guns by Glenn Beck.

Without going into depth, I will briefly address some concerns and issues I believe everyone should think about regardless of whether one is pro-gun or anti-gun. First, I support background checks. My concern is that two pieces of legislation, H.R. 8 and H.R. 1446. H.R. 8 is a "universal" background check bill that anti-gun legislators would argue must include a national a federal gun registry. H.R. 1446 would allow government bureaucrats to indefinitely delay lawful firearm transfers.

A federal gun registry is the first step toward gun confiscation. Carolyn D. Meadows states, "the pro-confiscation politicians are well-funded. Billionaires like George Soros and Michael Bloomberg gave more money to anti-Second Amendment politicians in 2020 alone than most families will make in a lifetime."[196] Frank Miniter says, "the delay of lawful firearm transfers could be used as an end-run around the U.S. Constitution, as a right that's indefinitely delayed is a right denied."[197]

---

[195] ibid.

[196] Billionaire Money Backs Gun Control, Meadows, Carolyn D., America's 1st Freedom, April 2021.

[197] Two Scary Years for Freedom, Miniter, Frank, America's 1st Freedom, May 2021.

Red flag laws allow law enforcement to take possession of a person's firearms if the person is accused of being a danger to themselves or others. This sounds good on the surface and has the potential to prevent mass shootings. However, the language of these laws is extremely important. Mike Wood reports, "as they currently exist, red flag laws allow the state to confiscate property and violate individual rights without the benefit of constitutionally protected due process. Since red flag hearings are conducted ex parte (done in the interest of one party only), the subject receives no prior warning that charges are being levied against them, is unable to confront their accuser and is denied the opportunity to defend themselves. Our legal system operates on the principle that all parties are innocent until proven guilty, but under red flag laws, the accused are assumed to be guilty from the start and required to prove their innocence. Worse yet, there is no requirement for compelling evidence before charges are levied – a mere accusation, even unsubstantiated, is enough to trigger the suspension of fundamental civil rights."[198] That means a disgruntled neighbor or worker could trigger the law simply by saying you are "dangerous."

Dick Fairburn suggests, "red flag orders should be a tool available to law enforcement but VERY difficult to obtain without police participation. This would help prevent the use of this powerful tool for retaliation or intimidation reasons. Similarly, filing a red flag request using false information should be a crime."[199]

I hear the term "common sense gun laws" but most of the suggested laws I hear about do not make much sense other than whatever benefit is gained from the political blather. The assault weapon ban most frequently references the AR-15. The AR-15 is not an assault weapon; it is a semi-automatic rifle. It is a powerful rifle, but it is not an assault weapon. Assault weapons are fully automatic rifles – machine guns if you prefer that terminology. For an assault rifle think AK-47 and M-16. Limiting magazine capacity to ten rounds does not help much. It takes about 1.5-2 seconds to change a magazine and 3-4 seconds to shoot ten rounds. Also, repealing gun manufacturers' immunity from liability is like holding the

---

[198] Opinion: The dangers posed by red flag laws, Wood, Mike, Police 1, October 30, 2019.
[199] ibid.

automobile manufacturer liable for a drunk driver going the wrong way on a one-way street and killing someone.

There is a Biden-Harris action I support and that is stopping the proliferation of ghost guns. Ghost guns are made at home usually from kits available through gun dealers or online vendors. The guns to not have serial numbers, are untraceable, are highly trafficked to Mexico and are increasingly use in criminal activities.

There are some measures that could be taken to make us a bit safer without infringing on the rights of legitimate gun owners. David Holahan, in his review of Ioan Grillo's book, Blood Gun Money: How America Arms gangs and Cartels, suggests reporting all sales of .50 caliber rifles to the ATF as this weapon was designed for combat, is accurate to 2,000 yards, and can penetrate structures and destroy light armored vehicles. He also suggests limiting the number of firearms a person can buy at one time. However, Wayne LaPierre states, "there are about 25,000 violent crimes a week in the United States. The 911 calls are chilling. The statistics are numbing. The innocent are being preyed upon. Everyone knows it. Who is more responsible for protecting our lives and the lives of our loved ones than we are? Why should we give up our right to survive?"[200]

Politicians are abdicating their responsibility by refusing to arrest, prosecute and incarcerate violent criminals. Kamala Harris, now Vice President Harris, helped raise money to bail out rioters and looters. We are creating a culture of irresponsibility. The focus needs to be on "bad" people – not "good" people. What bothers me most about those calling for gun control and confiscation is that they are rich, live in gated and safe communities, and are protected by people with guns – police and bodyguards.

July 6, 2020, Compared to 9/11

I am fed-up to my eyeballs with Senator Schumer and other Democratic lawmakers calling for a "9/11-style commission" to investigate the siege of the Capitol on January 6, 2021. In her Wall Street Journal commentary

---

[200] NRA Fights For Truth And Justice, LaPierre, Wayne, America's 1st Freedom, April 2021.

on May 28, 2021, Debra Burlingame reminds us that on 9-11-2001 "more than 3,000 children never saw their parents again. On January 6, Congress returned within hours." George Will recently said, "I would like to see Jan. 6 burned into the American mind as firmly as 9/11, because it was that scale of a Shock to the system. Burlingame continued saying, "the attempt to reconfigure the 'domestic terrorist' narrative to fit the horrifying story of September 11, 2001, is profoundly disheartening. These two events are fundamentally different in nature, scope, and consequences. Mentioning them in the same breath not only diminishes the horror of what happened on 9/11; it tells a false story to the generation of Americans who are too young to remember that day 20 years ago."

Debra Burlingame says there have been real terrorist attacks on the Capitol. "In 1971 the Weather Underground, a Marxist-Leninist terrorist group whose goal was the overthrow of the U.S. government through violent, armed revolution, blasted a hole through the ceiling on the Senate side of the complex. It also bombed the Pentagon in 1972 and the State Department in 1975. In 1954, four Puerto Rican nationalists opened fire with automatic weapons from the House visitor gallery with members in the chamber for a quorum call. Five representatives were wounded. The perpetrators received sentences ranging from 50-75 years; one was released in 1978, and President Carter granted clemency to the others the following year. One week after the shooting, the House was back to business as usual. That was a time when more members of Congress had served in the military, and with the world still recovering from World War II, one doubts that anyone likened the attack to Pearl Harbor or the Battle of Iwo Jima."[201]

The events of July 6, 2021, are being investigated by the FBI and the Capitol Police and more than 2,000 criminal charges have been filed against 411 suspects[202]. The truth will come out if the politicians want it to come out. It is time for the hyper-partisan crap to stop!

---

[201] It's a Travesty to Compare the Capitol Siege to 9/11, Burlingame, Debra, Commentary, The Wall Street Journal, May 28, 2021.

[202] Here's what a sprawling investigtion has found about the Capitol riot arrests, Barrett, Devlin, Hauslohner, Abigail, Hsu, Spencer S., Still, Ashlyn, The Washington Post, May 13, 2021.

Requiring COVID-19 Vaccination

This is the third and final time I will address COVID-19, and it will be in the form of questions for which I have not been able to find credible answers:

1. Why do young people, especially children, need to be vaccinated?
2. Why do the millions of people who have had the disease need to be vaccinated?
3. Can IgG antibody tests be used to avoid vaccinating people who have had COVID-19?
4. There is evidence of increased incidence of myocarditis in young people (especially men and boys) getting the vaccination. Why the big push to vaccinate everyone when there are still unanswered questions?
5. Doesn't an immunity passport make more sense than a vaccine passport?
6. Why do college students and staff that have had the disease need to be vaccinated?
7. Big pharma has made billions with the vaccines, is money the driving force for everyone to be vaccinated?
8. We now hear talks about the potential need for booster shots. Is that science or just a way for big pharma to make more money?
9. Will the government and the mainstream media ever accept the truth about the Wuhan Lab?
10. Why should President Biden be allowed to give pharmaceutical company's patents away? The government should not be able to give intellectual property away.

Dr. Fauci, NIH, CDC, and Science

This pains me to say, but I do not trust anything coming out of the mouth of Dr. Anthony Fauci, the CDC, the NIH, or the government in general. I believe in science, but only good science. The problem is, how do we know if we are hearing only good science? We cannot trust our political leaders to tell us the truth – they only tell us what they want us to hear. The same goes for the media – they have lost all credibility because they are driven by politics, not facts. We have been lied to and misled on so many issues it may be impossible for credibility to be restored.

All we can do is research issues ourselves and decide what makes sense to us. Hopefully, if we do this for a few critical issues, we can identify a source or two that we can have at least a modicum of faith that they are telling the truth on issues we do not have the time or resources to investigate ourselves. I have some confidence in The New York Post, The Wall Street Journal, and the analysis done by Tucker Carlson on FOX news. For COVID-19 information I look to Dr. Scott W. Atlas, Dr. Alex Berenson & Dr. Jay Bhattacharya (they got everything right that Dr. Fauci got wrong) and on Constitutional issues I seek information from Mark Levin and Alan Dershowitz. However, I do not rely solely on those sources. I still try to find original documents, scientific papers, etc. to confirm or refute what is reported.

Court-Packing

President Biden has appointed a commission to study the idea of court-packing. Court-packing became an issue after President Trump appointed three justices to the Supreme Court creating a majority of conservative (originalist) justices. Some Democrat lawmakers have said President Trump "packed" the court. There is a difference between "packing" the court and "stacking" the court. President Trump had the opportunity to appoint three justices and "stacked" the court with more conservative justices than liberal justices. Had a Democrat president been in power and conservative justices retired, or died, you can be sure he/she would appoint liberal judges. Which party is in power when justices need to be replaced is just "the way the cookie crumbles" so to speak.

The debate today over Court-Packing is much different than court stacking. In 2021, the Democrats are suggesting the addition of four liberal justices so the liberal justices will outnumber the conservative justices. The next time the Republicans are in power, they could add justices to create a majority of conservatives. It is theoretically possible that over the years the Supreme Court could grow from the current 9 to 25, 50 or higher. It would become a powerful political weapon.

There have been recommendations that there be term limits for justices or that there should be staggered terms, much like the Senate. Under that scenario, justices would retire and be replaced during every president's tenure. There is no problem having open and honest discussions about ways to change the system, but it needs to be a long and profoundly serious process. Such an extreme change cannot be allowed to happen at the whim of a disgruntled political party because the Supreme Court is "unbalanced."

Healthcare

I do not support Medicare for all, or any other government controlled, socialist style healthcare program. I passionately believe the only way to control healthcare cost and quality is through a consumer driven competitive market system. I have written two books on the subject and refer you to my 2018 book entitled, It's All About Money and Politics: Winning the Healthcare War. Enough said.

Destruction of Religious Freedoms

Under the auspices of COVID-19, many churches and synagogues have been forced to lockdown for a year or more. We saw tens of thousands of BLM protesters last year destroy cities and gather whenever and wherever they chose. Newsmax reported, "in San Francisco the Roman Catholic archdiocese was slapped with a cease-and-desist order saying some churches violated a local ban on large outdoor gatherings."[203] This has far less to do with COVID-19 than it has to do with the movement to fundamentally transform America. The transformation of America to a socialist style of government requires the dismantling of religion and banishing GOD from the lips, minds, and hearts of the faithful.

---

[203] The far left has a dark dream, both Jews and Christians are in grave danger..., Newsmax, April 2, 2021.

David Horowitz, a Jew, names, "Barak Obama, Hillary Clinton, Joe Biden, Kamala Harris, Alexandria Ocasio-Cortez, Andrew Cuomo, and others as wanting a Godless society. They're totally cool if thousands want to riot in protest of Trump and break all COVID-19 rules. But if you want to go to church or synagogue – with social distancing – they want you arrested!"[204]

Judeo-Christian values are at the root of America's democracy and success. Lose those values and our freedoms perish. In fact, America perishes. I encourage you to read the book, <u>Dark Agenda</u>, by David Horowtiz if you want a deep dive into secular left's disdain for Christians.

Climate Change

In the 1970s Time Magazine warned us of global cooling and an imminent ice age. In the 1990s we heard about global warming. Conventional terminology today is "climate change." That term gives scientists a little more "wiggle room" as information changes. No one can dispute that the climate is changing. It has been changing for somewhere around 4.5 billion years and will continue to change for a few billion more without regard to what we mere mortals do. We humans, like the dinosaurs, are only temporary inhabitants of this planet and although we may be able to prolong our lives, we will never rule the Earth. It will do its "thing" and decide when it is time for us to go. I do think the cockroach will survive about anything the Earth can throw at it, but we will not.

There is no dearth of fodder to feast on proclaiming that climate change is the greatest threat to our lives, America, and the world. However, what you do not hear much about are the opposing arguments by those that do not believe climate change is an existential crisis. If you are not afraid of being called a "Climate Change Denier" you should avail yourself of some of the papers by the CO_2 Coalition (co2coalition.org). In a June 9, 2021, CO_2 Coalition statement, Dr. Richard Lindzen, professor emeritus of atmospheric science, Massachusetts Institute of Technology, says, "What historians will definitely wonder about in future centuries is how deeply flawed logic, obscured by shrewd and unrelenting propaganda, actually

---

[204] ibid.

enabled a coalition of powerful special interests to convince nearly everyone in the world that carbon dioxide from human industry was a dangerous, planet-destroying toxin." Wikipedia says the CO_2 Coalition claims are disputed by a majority of climate scientists, but that may be because it does not adhere to the popular narrative. However, it is important to understand both sides of any argument. Whether you take climate change seriously or not, we should do what we can to keep the planet climate friendly to us; however, we should not sacrifice America in the process.

The climate change focus today is on the reduction of carbon dioxide emissions. President Obama implemented many climate change programs including fuel economy standards for passenger cars and heavy-duty trucks, new energy efficiency standards for appliances and equipment, programs to reduce methane emissions, and reducing America's reliance in HFCs (Hydrofluorocarbons used in refrigerators, air conditioners, aerosols, etc.). His goal was to reduce carbon dioxide emissions from electrical power generation to 32 percent below 2005 levels by 2030. He also set a target to cut greenhouse gas emissions between 26 to 28 percent below 2005 levels by 2025.

President Biden has committed to reduce U.S. greenhouse gas emissions by half below 2005 levels by 2030. According to the Wall Street Journal, his 10-year plan "tees up sweeping new government controls over the economy of the kind you might see in one of Mr. Xi's (Xi Jinping, President of the People's Republic of China) five-year plans. Mr. Biden now has a 10-year version of central economic planning."[205] The Wall Street Journal continues," amid last year's Covid-19 lockdowns, greenhouse gas emissions fell to about 21% below 2005 levels. In other words, even with the economy shut down and a large share of the population stuck at home, the U.S. was less than halfway to Mr. Biden's goal."[206]

The U.S. accounts for less than 15% of global CO_2 emissions. China is the biggest emitter of CO_2 (28% of all global CO_2 emissions) and other big emitters are India, Russia and Japan. We are kidding ourselves to believe we have major influence on China, Russia or other countries that hate America. With all the focus on transportation, it only accounts for 23%

---

[205] Biden's 10-Year Climate Plan, The Editorial Board, The Wall Street Journal, Apirl 22, 2021.
[206] ibid.

of global emissions. According to the American Institute of Architects, building operations and building materials and construction contribute 40% and industry contributes 32% of the CO_2 emissions.[207]

There are CO_2 emissions that we can do little to control. For example, there are coal-seam fires (underground coal fires) burning around the world including Russia, India, South Africa and China, and they contribute an estimated 3% of the world's CO_2 emissions. Elizabeth Claire Alberts reports that CO_2 from California wildfires is about 25% more than the state's annual emissions from fossil fuels.[208] According to the United States Geological Survey, volcanos produce about 1% of the annual carbon emissions. These uncontrollable events represent a small fraction of the CO_2 emissions and are dwarfed by those caused by human activity. However, I do like to wonder about our government's reaction if Mother Earth decided to burp out a few hundred 1815 Tambora, Indonesia size volcanic eruptions in a single year.

I do take climate change seriously, but our politicians over-politicize everything and there is no reason to believe that they are not doing the same thing with climate change. President Biden wants to spend billions to install 500,000 electric vehicle charging stations throughout the country – that is four times the number of U.S. gas stations. Where will the charging stations go? He is also proposing $174 billion investment in electric vehicles. What impact will the conversion to electric vehicles have on the already fragile power grid?

If you are forced to drive an electric vehicle, the distance you can drive between charging stations is limited. Current electric vehicles can go 250-360 miles between charges. If you can find a level 3 DC fast charger it can take about 30 minutes to charge your car. It takes five minutes or less to fill a car's tank with gas. There are too many fundamental questions to be answered before rushing headlong into the President's agenda. The rapid conversion from gas to electric vehicles is more about government controlling more aspects of your life than combatting climate change. Like anything else in politics, follow the money!

---

[207] Architecture's Carbon Problem, Blueprint for Better, American Institute of Architects.
[208] Off the chart: CO_2 from California fires dwarf state's fossil fuel emissions, Alberts, Elizabeth Claire, Mongabay, September 18, 2020.

Wind turbines and solar panels are not the long-term solution for reducing the use of fossil fuels. According to Center for Climate and Energy Solutions, wind and solar provide about 10% of the U.S. energy and all renewable energy sources are projected to supply about 24% by 2030.

We need to be looking far beyond expansion of technologies we have today. Nuclear fusion is the process occurring inside the core of the Sun. The Navy has a patent for a compact nuclear fusion (that powers the Sun) reactor[209] and Lockheed Martin is working to develop a source of infinite energy. It is this type of advanced technologies that we should be investing in.

Filibuster

The filibuster has changed over time and today, in the U.S. Senate, a filibuster is a tactic employed by opponents of a proposed law to prevent a measure from being brought to a vote. The most common form of filibuster occurs when one or more senators attempt to delay or block a vote on a bill by extending debate on the measure.[210] It is mostly used by the minority party to slow or block the majority party's agenda. It takes 60 votes to override a filibuster.

I will not dwell on the pros and cons of the filibuster and only include it to illustrate the hypocrisy in Washington, D.C. The Democrats have become critical of the filibuster since they hold majorities in the House, the Senate and have President Biden in the White House. President Biden has called the filibuster a Jim Crow relic and that it should be removed. Here is the hypocrisy – the Democrats used it 327 times in 2020[211] while Donald Trump was President. Whether you are for or against the filibuster boils down to whether you are in the majority or the minority party.

---

[209] The Navy's Patent for a Compact Nuclear Fusion Reactor is Wild, Leman, Jennifer, Popular Mechanics, October 18, 2021.

[210] wikipedia.org.

[211] Democrats used filibuster 327 times, compared to only once by GOP in 2020, Miller, Andrew Mark, Washington Examiner, March 26, 2021.

Movies

This may seem like a strange topic to include in this book, but there are movies every student should see before graduating from high school. The students should read the books, but since most will not devote the hours necessary to read the books, I am listing movies that they can watch in a couple of hours. To fully understand America, there must be an appreciation for its history, both good and bad, and the sacrifices thousands made to preserve our freedoms and culture that define her. These movies include:

- The Patriot
- Roots – 1977 series
- Gone With the Wind
- Glory
- Gettysburg
- Dances With Wolves
- All Quiet on the Western Front
- Sergeant York
- Mr. Smith Goes to Washington
- The Grapes of Wrath
- Schindler's List
- Tora, Tora, Tora
- Saving Private Ryan
- To Kill a Mockingbird
- Atlas Shrugged
- The Help
- The Green Book

There are others of course, but this is a starting point. If you want your children to understand sacrifice and what made America exceptional, watching these movies with them is a good place to start.

Virtue

Vocabulary.com defines virtue as follows: "Virtue is the quality of being morally good. The word virtue comes from the Latin root, vir, for man. At first, virtue meant manliness or valor, but over time it settled into the sense of moral excellence.

God assists us in living the moral life through the church. The church gives us rules to live by to lead a moral life – the Ten Commandments, for example. It is the rules that are the problem today. People do not want to be told what to do and not to do.

According to a March 2021 Gallop poll, "America's membership in church, synagogue or mosque has declined at leat one percent each year – dropping from 70% in 1998 to an all-time low of 47% by 2020. Before 1998, church membership had remained steady as far back as 1937. With more than 100 churches in America closing every week, where has our religion gone?"[212] Norris continues, "Besides the usual suspects of yard sales, the mall and sporting events, Shadi Hamid suggests a more disturbing answer to that question in a March 10, 2021, article in The Atlantic called, 'America Without God.' Hamid's article argues that there is 'a suspicious connection between the decline in religious faith and today's rising ideological intensity.' He further suggests that our faith is a limited quantity. So, as we've invested more energy into our political ideals, we've become less faithful to our places of worship."[213]

It is rare that I read or hear anything in the mainstream media about morality and virtue. What I do read and hear is hate-filled dialogue between Republicans and Democrats, between Socialists and Capitalists, between prolife and prochoice groups, Second Amendment rights and gun control advocates, and vitriolic comments about President Trump and President Biden. I must ask, has America lost its moral compass?

In the Federalist Papers, Samuel Adams wrote, "While the people are virtuous, they cannot be subdued; but when once they lose their virtue then they will be ready to surrender their liberties to the first external or internal invader." Is America surrendering to BLM, antifa, cancel culture,

---

[212] Wondering where has all our religion gone?, Burkes, Norris, Lafayett Journal and Courier, May 15, 2121.
[213] ibid.

LGBTQ, the claims of systemic racism and white supremacy? The answer is up to you!

Facebook and Smartphones

It was in 2006 or 2007 that my wife and I were in Florida attending a university professor's presentation about smartphones and Facebook. She was extolling what a wonderful vehicle it would become enabling people to easily stay in contact continuously sharing comments, pictures, etc. During the question & answer session that followed, my wife asked, "would this technology diminish personal, face to face interactions and thus damage relationships?" The professor's response was, "We're working on that."

Now that we are 15 years or so beyond my wife's extremely astute question, we now know the answer. Yes, social media and the smartphone have some nice features, but they have destroyed many relationships. People walk around with their faces glued to their smart phone not even recognizing people they meet on the street. Dinners and other events are interrupted by the all-important text, email, or phone call. People cannot get away from work and the school bullying does not end when the school bell rings, it continues throughout the evening, night, and weekend. Technology is the primary tool of cancel culture. I hear talk about a smart phone app for tracking those with COVID-19 vaccinations. If big tech (read federal government) can track our vaccinations it can track everything we do. It reminds me of Big Brother and the telescreen in Orwell's 1984.

I am now of the opinion that no child under age 18 should have a smartphone. If they need a communication device for safety, calling home, etc., a flip-phone will serve that purpose. If they need to investigate something on the internet, computers will do the job. Let people interact face-to-face again. Let us say "hell-o" when meeting someone on the street again. Let us focus on dinner, or whatever we are doing, rather than that little box that is controlling our lives.

CHAPTER FOURTEEN

Election Integrity

The Oxford dictionary define integrity as: 1) the quality of being honest and having strong moral principles; moral uprightness and 2) the state of being whole and undivided. Upholding territorial integrity and national sovereignty.

The Electoral Knowledge Network states that election integrity must be "professional, impartial, and transparent in its preparation and administration throughout the electoral cycle." In addition to the definitions and statements above, I will add my own plain language definition of election integrity. Election integrity is when:

- Every citizen with the right to vote has a fair and reasonable opportunity to exercise that right.
- The identity of every voter is verified.
- Voter rolls are purged of those who are no longer eligible to vote in each precinct/state.
- Those voting by mail shall request a ballot – no mass mailing of ballots.
- There are no changes to state voting laws/rules after the first ballot is cast.
- Vote harvesting is prohibited.
- People cannot be paid or incentivized to vote.
- There are severe penalties for anyone found guilty of vote/election tampering.

- All ballots are secured with documented chain-of-custody and counted with close monitoring by all political parties.
- Vote counting and reporting is completed within 24 hours of the close of voting.
- Tabulating machines are banned unless wireless connectivity capability is disabled.

The Democrats have introduced bills H.R.1 and S.1 to seize control of election rules nationwide. J. Christian Adams reports, "H.R.1 packs into one 791-page bill every bad idea about how to run elections and mandates that the states must adopt – the very things that made the election of 2020 such a mess. It includes all of the greatest hits of 2020: Mandatory mail ballots, ballots without postmarks, late ballots and voting in precincts where you don't live. It includes so many bad ideas that no publication has satisfactory space to cover all of them. The Senate companion bill, S.1, might be even worse."[214] Adams continues with the following points:

- H.R.1 dispenses with the idea that an American should register to vote.
- States would be blocked by H.R.1 from signature verification procedures.
- H.R.1 rigs the system for any lawsuits challenging the constitutionality of the law.
- H.R.1 prohibits states from conducting list maintenance on the voter rolls.
- H.R.1 would do away with actual voter registration and instead make the voter rolls merely a copy of anyone already on a government list.
- H.R.1 and S.1 will force states to push ballots into the mail. States may not enact identification requirements of any form for those requesting a ballot.
- States would be blocked from signature verification procedures.
- Unlimited ballot harvesting is guaranteed.

---

[214] If You Thought The 2020 Elections Were Chaotic, Just Wait, Adams, J. Christian, Gatestone, February 8, 2021.

There is more, including Constitutional issues, but that is enough to make the point – everything that led many to believe the 2020 presidential election was stolen is included in the two bills.

In its "Oppose Voter ID Legislation – Fact Sheet, the American Civil Liberties Union (ACLU) contains the following:

- "Voter ID laws deprive many voters of their right to vote, reduce participation, and stand in direct opposition to our country's trend of including more Americans in the democratic process. Many Americans do not have one of the forms of identification states accept for voting. These voters are disproportionately low-income, racial and ethnic minorities, the elderly, and people with disabilities. Such voters more frequently have difficulty obtaining ID, because they cannot afford or cannot obtain the underlying documents that are a prerequisite to obtaining a government-issued photo ID card."
- "A 2014 GAO study found that strict photo ID laws reduce turnout by 2-3 percentage points."
- "Voter ID laws reduce turnout among minority voters."
- "Voter ID laws are a waste of taxpayer dollars. Texas spent nearly $2 million on voter education and outreach efforts following passage of its Voter ID law."

I have a couple of questions for the ACLU: What about my right to have assurance that only American Citizens vote to select our president? What is wrong with Texas spending money for voter education and outreach? I am sympathetic with those that have difficulty in obtaining a valid picture ID. On August 14, 2013, in the Washington Examiner, Ashe Schow shared a list of 24 things that require you to prove your identity:

- Buying alcohol
- Buying cigarettes
- Opening a bank account
- Applying for food stamps
- Applying for welfare
- Applying for Medicaid/Social Security

- Applying for unemployment or a job
- Rent/buy a house, apply for a mortgage
- Drive/buy/rent a car
- Get on an airplane
- Get married
- Purchase a gun
- Adopt a pet
- Rent a hotel room
- Apply for a hunting license
- Apply for a fishing license
- Buy a cell phone
- Visit a casino
- Pick up a prescription
- Hold a rally or protest
- Donate blood
- Buy an "M" rated video game
- Purchase nail polish at CVS
- Purchase certain cold medicines

I can now add getting a COVID-19 vaccination to that list – in fact, I had to show mine twice for both my first and second shots.

It is extremely difficult for me to believe that with all the things listed above, plus more, that require proof of identity to participate in, that requiring proof of identity to vote is unreasonable. Claiming that minorities are not smart enough or are incapable of getting a voter ID is the most demeaning thing they can be accused of. Regarding immigrants that have a language barrier impeding their ability to obtain voter ID, as harsh as it sounds, they should earn the right to vote by assimilating to America, our laws, our customs and our language.

Today we have corporations, Coca-Cola, and Delta for example, weighing in on state voter laws. These corporations should stick to selling soft drinks and flying airplanes and leave voting laws and politics to the people of the states. We need a country of, by and for the people – not a corporatocracy.

Every issue in this book is affected by the politicians we place in office. There is nothing more important to the future of America than assuring those politicians are placed in office by elections that all can believe are fair, honest, and above reproach regarding the integrity of all votes cast.

ACTIONS

1. Volunteer to register voters.
2. When registering voters, ask if they have voter ID or need assistance in obtaining it.
3. Talk to your state senators and representatives to assure your state's voter ID laws are fair and reasonable.
4. Ascertain what your state is doing to clean up voter rolls and, if possible, volunteer to help.
5. Volunteer to be a poll worker during elections.
6. Volunteer to be an observer during the counting of ballots.
7. Vote!

Conclusion

I remember America when we had freedom – freedom to think what we want; freedom to express what we believe; freedom to do what we want; freedom to go where we want. I remember a country where people respected the law and the police. I remember a country that had made great progress toward judging a person by the content of their character and not by the color of their skin. The America I remember is being cancelled right before our eyes.

America is in the midst of being fundamentally transformed into a very different country. It began, in silence, decades ago, but was recognized as an actual movement when, in an October 2008 campaign speech, Barack Obama said, "We are five days away from fundamentally transforming the United States of America." When someone says they want to "fundamentally transform America," they are actually saying, "I hate America."

The elite, left-leaning activists, corporate leaders, and the political left are speaking "I HATE AMERICA" loud and clear, not only with their words, but through their actions. Today, our southern border is wide open with an estimated 1,000,000+ illegal aliens having entered the country between January and mid-June 2021. The FBI and IRS are politicized. Our schools are teaching our children to hate each other, just as schools in China, Russia, and North Korea do. Rather than being united, we are being divided and told we should be ashamed of being white because of something our ancestors did more than a century ago. If we say something that rejects the "ruling class" dogma, our speech is cancelled by big tech, the media and those in the political majority. If we are white and reject the "ruling class," we are labeled as racist, xenophobic, and even domestic terrorists and anarchists. People lose their jobs because of something they said, or wrote, years ago and many are afraid to say what they think out of fear of reprisals. The government is growing and injecting itself into every aspect of our lives and is planning to redistribute trillions through massive taxation and spending. We have BLM flags flying over our embassies and mothers are now "birthing persons."

I will conclude with what Thomas Paine wrote on December 19, 1776:

"THESE are the times that try men's souls. The summer soldier and the sunshine patriot will, in this crisis, shrink form the service of their county; but he that stands it now, deserves the love and thanks of man and woman.

Tyranny, like hell, is not easily conquered; yet we have this consolation with us, that the harder the conflict, the more glorious the triumph.

What we obtain too cheap, we esteem too lightly: it is dearness only that gives everything its value. Heaven knows how to put a proper price upon its goods; and it would be strange indeed if so celestial an article as FREEDOM should not be highly rated."

Are you a summer soldier or sunshine patriot or a member of the cavalry riding to the rescue of freedom, liberty, and justice? Will you allow America to be cancelled or will you help her to survive? The choice is yours and yours alone.

May God bless America!

Other References

- China's Word for Woke American Liberals: "BAIZOU," Carlson, Tucker, FOX News.
- Biden: 'Erratic' Trump shouldn't get intel briefings, Collins, Michael, USA Today, February 2, 2021.
- WOKE, Wikipedia, https://en.m.wikipedia.org/wiki/Woke.
- Counting Regulations: An Overview of Rulemaking, Types of Federal Regulation, and Pages in the Federal Register, Congressional Research Service, September 3, 2019.
- The Growth of Government in America, Moore, Stephen, Foundation for Economic Education, April 1, 1993.
- Joe Biden's executive orders and actions, Ballotpedia, March 20, 2021.
- US Rep. Greene says 'morons' cost her posts, Fram, Alan and Slodysko, Brian, jconline.com, February 6, 2021.
- McCarthy Warns Dems of Repercussions from Kicking Rep. Greene Off Committees, trumptrainnews.com/, February 2, 2021.
- Twitter warns that Rokita tweet might spur violence, Madgaleno, Johnny, Indianapolis Star, February 20, 2021.
- Facebook assailed for Aussie news ban, Ortutay, Barbara and Arbel, Tali, Associated Press, February 20, 2021.
- Restoring the Rule of Law Through a Fair, Humane, and Workable Immigration System, Jawetz, Tom, Center for American Progress, July 22, 2019.
- How Many Rules and Regulations Do Federal Agencies Issue?, Crews, Clyde Wayne Jr., Forbes, August 15, 2017.
- How the Left Is Working Overtime to Silence Your Voice, Purdum, Don, RightWing.org, 2021.

- Fla. Lawmakers challenge Silicon Valley 'censorship,' Calva, Bobcaina, Associated Press, February 2, 2021.
- Migrants go free without court dates, Spagat, Elliott, Associated Press, April 2, 2021.
- Guatemala Takes Emergency Measures Amid Immigration Surge, TargetLiberty.org, April 2, 2021.
- Ted Cruz Identifies Three Biden Decisions that Provoked 'Entirely Preventable Border Crisis,' Louder With Crowder, April 2, 2021.
- White House Plan on Migrant Children Brings Concern Among Federal Officials, McCarthy, Charlie, Newsmax, April 1, 2021.
- Why Don't Immigrants Apply for Citizenship?, Fact Sheet, American Immigration Council, November 25, 2019.
- Bring back public shame about racism, Demings, Val, USA Today, March 23, 2021.
- Jucicial Watch Sues for Records of Pelosi Call with Pentagon Chief, Judicial Watch, March 9, 2021.
- Citizenship hopes lift immigrants, Taxin, Amy, Roberson, Jeff and Aleman, Marcos, Associated Press, April 3, 2021.
- What? Biden Spends Enough of Tax-Payers' Money on Migrants to Buy Them Houses, patriottruthnews.com/latest-news/what-biden-spends-enough-of-tax-payers-money-on-migrants-to-buy-them-houses/, March31, 2021.
- The comical side of 'cancel culture,' Paulson, Ken, USA Today, March 11, 2021.
- Study faults health disparities, Alltucker, Ken, USA Today, February 12, 2021.
- CDC moving nation's pupils closer to normal, Stobbe, Mike, Associated Press, March 20, 2021.
- Schools weigh seating students closer, Binkley, Collin, Associated Press, U.S. News and World Report, March 16, 2021.
- Loosen rules on reopening schools, Henderson, Dr. Tara O., Gandhi, Dr. Monica, Hoeg, Dr. Tracy Beth and Johnson, Dr. Daniel, USA Today, March 10, 2021.
- Masks in America: Hiding, revealing, transforming, Looper, Shayne, Journal and Courier, February 6, 2021.

- Enough could be immune in June, Siegel, Dr. Marc, USA Today, March 31, 2021.
- Experts Are Ruining the Constitution, Purdum, RightWing.org, 2021.
- Don't expect a Hollywood ending, Anthony, Ted, Associated Press, March 26, 2021.
- 'Very reassuring': Vaccines found highly effective in real-world US study, Stobbe, Mike, Associated Press, March 29, 2021.
- What Rand Paul gets wrong – and right- on masks, Catanese, David, Lexington Herald Leader, March 24, 2021.
- Hunger crisis persists throughout US, Snow, Anita, Santana, Rebecca and Choi, Candice, Lafayette Journal and Courier, April 3, 2021.
- Will unvaccinated people be shunned?, Craven, Scott, azcentral, March 10, 2021.
- Study of nearly 2,000 Marine recruits reveals asymptomatic SARS-CoV-2 transmission, The Mount Sinai Hospital/Mount Sinai School of Medicine, Science Daily, November 11, 2020.
- The Media Have Brainwashed People, Kaiser Health News, April 1, 2021.
- Cuomo ripped for count on nursing home deaths, Hill, Michael, Villeneuve, Marina and Peltz, Jennifer, Associated Press, February, 14, 2021.
- Bundy builds militia network on COVID-19 backlash, Read, Richard, Los Angeles Times Tribune News Service, February, 14, 2021.
- COVID-19 surge helped to create herd immunity, Karlamangla, Soumya and Lin II, Rong-Gong, Los Angeles Times Tribune News Service, February 22, 2021.
- Prioritizing for vaccine has no easy blueprint, Rudavsky Shari, Indianapolis Star, February 12, 2021.
- Biden rejects 'America First' plan, Madhani, Aamer, Associated Press, February 20, 2021.
- Distrust rooted in lies, loss, Hassanein, Nada, USA Today, March 17, 2021.
- Ban on renter evictions extended, Khalil, Ashraf, Associated Press, abc News, March 29, 2021.
- FBI checks waived at border sites, Merchant, Nomaan, Lafayette Journal and Courier, March 29, 2021.

- <u>Hooked: Food, Free Will, and How the Food Giants Exploit Our Addictions</u>, Moss, Michael, March, 2021.
- Anti-free speech, pro-propaganda: How Biden's media czar endorsed decades-old tradition of indoctrinating Americans, Klarenberg, Kit, RT.com, November 18, 2020.
- What Georgia's new voting law really does – 9 facts, Brewster, Adam, Huey-Burns, Caitlin, CBS News, April 7, 2021.
- Unheralded slave had notable life, Luciano, Phil, Peoria Journal Star, February 8, 2021.
- List of landmark African-American legislation, Wikipedia.
- Systemic racism Refuted Long Ago, Just Don't Tell the Left, Reagan, Michael with Shannon, Michael R., Newsmax, July 21, 2020.
- Thomas Sowell: Idea of 'systemic racism' a lie that has 'no meaning' and is reminiscent of Nazi propaganda, Miller, Andrew Mark, Washington Examiner, July 13, 2020.
- What Systemic Racism Means And The Way It Harms Communities, NPR, July 1, 2020.
- When Everything is 'Systemic Racism,' People Will Tune Out the Term, Welch, Matt, Reason, April 4, 2021.
- 5 Simple Reasons to Stop Calling My Husband "SuperDad," Kaylene, autisticmama.com.
- The Fight for Transgender Athletes' Right to Compete, Benton, Emilia, Runner's World, March 18, 2021.
- LGBTQ+ Suicide Statistics Show Greater Risk Among Young Teens, Newport Academy, May 6, 2019.
- What It Means to Be Transgender, Fields, Lisa, WEBMD ARCHIVES, July 27, 2017.
- Lesbian, Gay, Bisexual, and Transgender Health, HealthyPeople.gov.
- Nikki Haley: Biden's Transgender Order 'Attack on Women's Rights,' Reyner, Solange, Newsmax, February 8, 2021.
- The fight for the future of transgender athletes, Hobson, Will, The Washington Post, April 15, 2021.
- The Black Lives Matter foundation raised $90 million in 2020, and gave almost a quarter of it to local chapters and organization, Morava, Maria and Andrew, Scottie, CNN, February 25, 2021.

- Black Lives Matter fundraising handled by group with convicted terrorist on its board, Dunleavy, Jerry, Washington Examiner, June 25, 2020.
- Marxist BLM leader buys $1.4 million home in ritzy LA enclave, Vincent, Isabel, New York Post, April 10, 2021.
- Biden Orders Feds: Ensure Transgenders Access to 'the Restroom, the Locker Room, or School Sports' of Their Choice, CBSNews.com Staff, January 22, 2021.
- Photos show the 'autonomous zone' set up by protesters in Seattle, which forbids police from entering has enraged Trump, insider.com, June 11, 2020.
- Shocking Truths About What Protests Cost You, DePietro, Andrew, Taxes 101, March 29, 2017.
- The police officer who fatally shot 13-year-old Adam Toledo was listed as a victim on an incident report. One law-enforcement expert said it's 'an old cop trick meant to muddy the murky waters., Frias, Lauren, Insider, April 19, 2021.
- Ma'Khia Bryant argued about housekeeping before fatal police shooting, foster parent says, Sanchez, Morales, Mark and Carroll, Jason, CNN, April 22, 2021.
- REPORT: Hypocrite Maxine Waters Sought Police Escort to Cop-Bashing BLM Rally, Contributing Author, headlingusa.com, April 20, 2021.
- Nancy Pelosi Clarifies Her Criticized Reaction to Derek Chauvin Verdict: 'George Floyd Should Be Alive,' Chamlee, Virginia, news.yahoo.com, April 21. 2021.
- Joe and Jen's Police Narrative, The Editorial Board, The Wall Street Journal, April 22, 2021.
- FNC's Carlson: 'Maxine Waters Is Someone Who Supports Mob Violence – She Always Supported, We Have Known This,', Poor, Jeff, April 20, 2021.
- Trump: LeBron James' Tweets on Teen's Death Are 'Racist Rants,' Fitzgerald, Sandy, Newsmax, April 23, 2021.
- Ronald Reagan and Personal Responsibility, New York Times, March 5, 1987.

- BLM Founder Defends Massive Home Buying Despite Past Marxist Claims, The Liberty Revolution, March 23, 2021.
- Tracking Chicago shooting victims, Chicago Tribune, www.chicagotribune.com>data>ct-shooting-victims.
- Most Chicago homicide victims over the past decade are Black, police data show, Casiano, Louis, Pagones, Stephanie, FOX News, June 23, 2020.
- How to Have More Police Shootings, Jenkins, Holman, W. Jr., The Wall Street Journal, April 23, 2021.
- Anticop Movement Wants Road Anarchy Too, MacDonald, Heather, The Wall Street Journal, April 22, 2021.
- Firearms Transaction Record, U.S. Department of Justice.
- GOP Reps. Urge ATF to Investigate Whether Hunter Biden Lied on Gun Background Check, Downey, Caroline, National Review, April 27, 2021.
- Over 300 rioters charged with crimes committed during BLM protests, Department of Justice, September 25, 2020.
- What we know about the "unprecedented" U.S. Capitol riot arrests, CBS News, April 26, 2021.
- FBI: No Firearms Were Found in the US Capitol During the January 6 Riot, Zimmerman, Dan, March 3, 2021.
- Officer Cleared In The Shooting Death Of Ashli Babbitt During Capitol Riot, Jones, Dustin, Twitter, April 14, 2021.
- There shouldn't be a double standard for law & order: Devine, Devine, Miranda, New York Post, February 21, 2021.
- In a nation founded on whiteness, how to really discuss it?, Hajela, Deepti, Lafayette Journal and Courier, March 28, 2021.
- Chauvin Trial Judge: Maxine Waters' Statement 'May Overturn This Whole Trial,' https://trueconservativeshub.com/2021/04/20/chauvin-trial-judge-maxine-waters-statement-mayh-overturn-this-whole-trial/.
- Americans can support the police while also supporting police reform, Caldwell, Gianno, The New York Post, April 24, 2021.
- U.S. Education Spending and Performance vs. The World, Rossier Staff, USC Rossier, February 9, 2011.
- Spending Per Pupil Increased for Sixth Consecutive Year, U.S. Census Bureau, May 11, 2020.

- Marc Lamont Hill shuts down GOP's Vernon Jones on critical race theory, Inman, DeMicia, news.yahoo.com, May 5, 2021.
- Equity Isn't Equality, Andrews, Douglas, The Patriot Post, January 27, 2021.
- Equality vs. equity in Joe Biden's America, Leonard, John, American Thinker, December 25, 2020.
- Biden pushes for 'equity' over 'equality.' Here's the difference – and why it matters, Aldridge, Bailey, McClatchy, February 1, 2021.
- Don't Fall for the Equality/Equity Trap, Stanton, Glenn T., The Daily Citizen, February 18, 2021.
- Equity vs. Equality: What's the Difference in the Workplace?, Weyrauch, Emily, Blog, January 22, 2021.
- How Educational Equity Benefits All Students, Summers, Andi, From the Blog, September 25, 2019
- TSC Advances Diversity and Inclusion, Tippecanoe School Corporation Newsletter, Lafayette, Indiana, Spring 2021.
- Youth Pay a High Price for Covid Protection, Hooper, Charles L. and Henderson, David R., The Wall Street Journal, May 3, 2021.
- The Schools Aren't Really Open, The Editorial Board, The Wall Street Journal, May 2, 2021.
- Many Wisconsin schools stayed open during pandemic: report, Beyer, Elizabeth, Wisconsin Associated Press, March 20, 2021.
- U.S. Students Show No Improvement in Math, Reading, Science on International Exam, Camera, Lauren, U.S. New and World Report, December 3, 2019.
- Florida's School Voucher Expansion, The Editorial Board, The Wall Street Journal, April 27, 2021.
- Rethinking School Discipline, U.S. Department of Education, January 8, 2014.
- Why Is Family Involvement in Education Important?, Bogenschneider, Karen, Gross, Beth and Johnson, Carol, Policy Institute For Family Impact Seminars, June 2004.
- Remote Kindergarten Could Affect Children 'for Their Lifetime,' Bauerlein, Valerie, The Wall Street Journal, June 9, 2021.
- Classroom Chaos in the Name of Racial Equity Is a Bad Lesson Plan, Riley, Jason L., The Wall Street Journal, June 12, 2021.

- Do We Need the Department of Education?, Murray, Charles, Imprimis vol. 4. No. 1, January 2012.
- U.S. Department of Education, Fiscal Year 2021, Budget Summary.
- Family Involvement in Education: How Important Is It? What Can Legislators Do?, Bogenschneider, Karen and Johnson, Carol, Policy Institute for Family Impact Seminars, February 2004.
- America Needs History and Civics Education to Promote Unity, Riley, Richard W., Alexander, Lamar, Duncan, Arne, King, John, Paige, Rod and Spellings, Margaret, The Wall Street Journal, March 1, 2021.
- Discipline in Schools, Kelly, Melissa, Thoushtco.com, May 16, 2020.
- 7 ways to Repair the Public Education System, Hollis, Anya, Huffington Post, March 23, 2016.
- Biden's 'infrastructure' plan is really a massive push to unionize the US workforce, McCaughey, Betsy, The New York Post, May 4, 2021.
- Monthly Child Tax Credit Payments to Start July 15, CNBC, May 27, 2021.
- A Bad Infrastructure Bargain, The Editorial Board, The Wall Street Journal, May 21, 2021.
- Audits eyed for infrastructure cash, Freking, Kevin and Gordon, Marcy, Lafayette Journal and Courier, May 16, 2021.
- List of amendments to the United States Constitution, https://en.m.wikipedia.org/wiki/List_of_amendments_to_the_United_States_Constitution.
- The Constitution: Amendments 11-17, National Archives.
- How To Legally Quote Song Lyrics in Your Stories, Books and Articles, Lovine, John, TheStartup, Aprils5, 2020.
- Study: Very Few Rioters With Ties To 'Right-Wing' Groups During Jan. 6 Events, https://patriottruthnews.com/latest-news-very-few-rioters-with-ties-to-right-wing-groups-during-jan-6-events/.
- Two sides to Biden's $15 wage proposal, Wiesman, Paul, Associated Press, February 20, 2021.
- Facebook's Secret Rulebook Confounds Penalized Users, Grind, Kristen, The Wall Street Journal, May 5, 2021.
- The Supply-Side Jobs Slowdown, The Editorial Board, The Wall Street Journal, May 8, 2021.

- Debate Rages Over Enhanced Benefits, Weber, Lauren and Haddon Heather, The Wall Street Journal, May 8, 2021.
- Job Openings Reach Record as Hiring Slows, Morath, Eric, The Wall Street Journal, May 12, 2021.
- Biden's Free-College Plan Meets Resistance, Mitchell, Josh, The Wall Street Journal, May 16, 2021.
- The Great Student-Loan Income Transfer, The Editorial Board, The Wall Street Journal, April 15, 2021.
- Education Dept. reverses rule on loan forgiveness, Feldman, Carole, Associated Press, March 19, 2021.
- Newly Released Interview Reveals Biden's Plan To Pass Gun Ban, bearingarms.com, February 8, 2021.
- Can Biden Take Your Rights With the Stroke of a Pen?, America's 1st Freedom, May 2021.
- Biden's Nominees Signal Coming Attack On Gun Rights, Ouimet, Jason, America's 1st Freedom, March 2021.
- Covid-19 Shot Can Be a Job Requirement, Morath, Eric and Cambon, Sarah Chaney, The Wall Street Journal, May 28, 2021.
- Wuhan Lab Theory Is a Media Warning, Jenkins, Holman W. Jr., The Wall Street Journal, May 28, 2021.
- Biden's Architecture of Power, Panero, James, The Wall Street Journal, May 26, 2021.
- The Malarkey Zone, Bill O'Reilly.com, February 7, 2021.
- How Democratic Party fundraiser and former ambassador Suizi LeVine came to run Washington state's embattled unemployment system, Brunner, Jim and Malone, Patrick, The Seattle Times, June 2, 2020.
- Biden Rewards Inauguration Donor with Huge Federal Contract, https://trumptrainnews.com, February 13, 2021.
- Adam Schiff rips Kevin McCarthy: 'He has no values,' Chaitin, Danile, The Washington Examiner, February 7, 2021.
- Forgetting Justice Marshall, The Editorial Board, The Wall Street Journal, May 25, 2021.
- Facebook's Lab-Leak About-Fact, The Editorial Board, The Wall Street Journal, May 27, 2021.

- El Salvador and Court-Packing Democrats, O'Grady, Mary Anastasia, The Wall Street Journal, May 9, 2021.
- Department of National Child Care, The Editorial Board, The Wall Street Journal, May 9, 2021.
- Biden's Vaccine Patent Theft, The Editorial Board, The Wall Street Journal, May 5, 2021.
- Federal government should not reform police, Lafayette Journal and Courier, May 16, 2021.
- Surprising Absolutely Everyone, CBS Issues Scathing Report on How Badly Biden betrayed Keystone Workers, Jones, Kip, westernjournal.com, February 5, 2021.
- US returns to Paris climate accord, Borenstein Seth and Knickmeyer, Ellen, Associated Press, February 21, 2021.
- Democrats have vigorously used the filibuster. It's pathetic they now won't pledge to protect it., Thiessen, Marc A., The Washington Post, January 26, 2021.
- H.R.1 Would Steamroll the Constitution, Rivkin, David B. Jr. and Snead, Jason, The Wall Street Journal, June 6, 2021.
- States End Enhanced Aid for the Jobless, McCormick, John and Cambon, Sarah Chaney, The Wall Street Journal, May 12, 2021.
- CEOs Lead America's New Great Awakening, Sonnenfeld, Jeffrey, The Wall Street Journal, April 15, 2021.
- Did Pelosi Reject Security Help at the Capitol on Jan. 6th?, Paladino, Joshua, headlineusa.com, February 15, 2021.
- Weakened voting security worries activists, Bajak, Frank, Lafayette Journal and Courier, February 7, 2021.
- Report highlights cyber risks to election system, Cassidy, Christina A., Associated Press, February 12, 2021.
- A Time Bomb for the 2022 Elections, The Editorial Board, The Wall Street Journal, May 14, 2021.
- The Facts on Florida's Election Law, The Editorial Board, The Wall Street Journal, May 22, 2021.
- Arizona Enacts Mail-Ballot Law, Corse, Alexa and Kamp, Jon, The Wall Street Journal, May 12, 2021.
- Breaking: Maricopa County Officials Deleted entire database from Voting Machines, Hale, Mark, Patriot Truth News, May 13, 2021.

- Kemp Defends Election Integrity Law Against Woke & Spineless Corporate CEOs, Contributing Author, headlineusa.com, April 2, 2021.
- Climate models fail in key test region, Whitehouse, Dr. David, Watts Up With That?, June 6, 2021
- Net-Zero Carbon Dioxide Emissions By 2050 Requires A New Nuclear Power Plant Every Day, Pielke, Roger, forbes.com, September 30, 2019.
- Florida's New Law Bars Twitter, Facebook and Others from Blocking Political Candidates, McKinnon, John D., The Wall Street Journal, May 25, 2021.
- Biden's Cradle-to-Grave Government, The Editorial Board, The Wall Street Journal, April 28, 2021.
- Biden's $6 Trillion Plan for Permanent Culture War, The Wall Street Journal, May 6, 2021.
- Biden's Economic Plan Would Redistribute Trillions and Expand Government, Schlesinger, Jacob M., The Wall Street Journal, April 29, 2021.
- Democrats Are Killing the American Dream, Henninger, Daniel, The Wall Street Journal, May 5, 2021.

www.ingramcontent.com/pod-product-compliance
Lightning Source LLC
Chambersburg PA
CBHW021413210526
45463CB00001B/355